Meeting Christ at his Table

Jonathan Edwards and the Lord's Supper

Meeting Christ at his Table

Jonathan Edwards and the Lord's Supper

David Luke

Volume 4

A Series of Treatises on Jonathan Edwards

JE Society Press

WWW.JESOCIETY.ORG

Paperback Edition May 7, 2023
ISBN 978-1-7379026-6-9

A publication of JESociety Press
Visit https://www.jesociety.org

For permission requests and inquiries,
Email: rob@jesociety.org
Web: www.jesociety.org

PRAISE FOR THIS VOLUME

'This learned and judicious treatment of Jonathan Edwards' doctrine of the Lord's Supper is now the place to begin for serious readers. It places Edwards' doctrine reliably in historical, practical, and theological context, helping students understand the reasons Edwards was ejected from his pulpit in Northampton—and helping Christians participate in this sacrament more faithfully and holily.'

Douglas A. Sweeney
Beeson Divinity School
Samford University

'Popular Evangelical thinking about the Lord's Supper is a paltry affair, to say the least. One way forward to a greater appreciation of this vital means of grace is a renewed consideration of how the Table was viewed by our spiritual forebears. In this regard, David Luke's fresh and ground-breaking study of Jonathan Edwards' eucharistic theology would be an excellent starting-point. Here we see that Edwards treasured the Lord's Supper not simply as a place of remembrance (the sole meaning assigned to the Table by far too many Evangelicals), but also as a covenant seal, a time of spiritual nourishment, and a vehicle of rich communion with Christ and with fellow believers. Highly recommended!'

Michael A.G. Haykin
Chair and Professor of Church History
The Southern Baptist Theological Seminary, Louisville, KY

'David Luke's work on Jonathan Edwards and the Lord's Supper opens up a significant and neglected dimension of Edwards' thought. Students of Edwards have often concentrated on the communion controversy in Northampton, as a result of which Edwards lost his job. Yet every two months Edwards preached sacrament sermons which concentrated on Jesus Christ, the work of redemption, and Christian experience. This volume is an excellent introduction to the variety of perspectives these sermons offered on this spiritual feast.'

Michael McClenahan
Professor of Systematic Theology
Union Theological College, Belfast

‘With meticulous attention to Edwards’ writings and to his sermons, both published and unpublished, David Luke examines all the pertinent issues, including the nature of the Supper and Christ’s presence in it, the manner in which communicants should participate in the sacrament and, of course, the qualifications for worthy participation. The study is thorough, yet readable and accessible, must-reading for Edwards specialists and for all with an interest in the theology of the Lord’s Supper and participation in it.’

David McKay
Professor of Systematic Theology, Ethics and Apologetics, Reformed Theological College, Belfast and minister of Shaftesbury Square Reformed Presbyterian Church

‘The subject of Edwards’ views on the Lord’s Supper has long been a matter of discussion, since it was his theology of Communion that largely led to the shocking events of the Northampton Church’s dismissal of America’s greatest theologian. However, in contemporary Edwardsean scholarship, most research has focused on the surprising fact that it happened rather than Edwards’ actual theology of the holy table. David Luke’s book on this topic fills a crucial hole here. Luke’s new book is short, sweeping, and imminently helpful. I personally benefited tremendously from this work, and had significant gaps in my own ignorance filled.’

Matthew Everhard
Pastor of Gospel Fellowship PCA
Valencia, Pennsylvania

‘In writing this little volume, David Luke has afforded a great gift to the Church. By carefully unpacking Edwards’ theological understanding of the Lord’s Supper as found in his sermons, miscellanies, and treatises, and then placing Edwards’ reflections into the wider context of Reformation and post-Reformation thought, Luke reveals both Edwards’ faithfulness to his heritage as well as his own rich doctrinal and devotional contributions. In so doing, he prompts us all to ponder anew the staggering breadth, and length, and depth, and height of this most holy Christian ordinance.’

Brandon James Crawford
Senior Pastor, Grace Baptist Church
Marshall, Michigan

In memory of my much-loved parents,

Elaine Luke (1937-2002)

John Luke (1925-2017)

Acknowledgments

My thanks must go to the management committee of the Irish Baptist College where I am a member of the faculty. The committee kindly granted me a sabbatical to work on this book which allowed me to focus on writing and made the task more enjoyable. I must also thank the faculty and staff of the college who kindly took on extra duties during my absence.

Thanks too to Robert L. Boss of the Jonathan Edwards Society Press who readily agreed to adopt this project. I appreciate Rob's input and help in producing the finished book.

Thanks to my very good friend David Middleton for providing the artwork for the cover.

Finally, thanks to my dearly loved wife, Elizabeth. Her support and encouragement have been unflinching throughout the project.

Contents

INTRODUCTION

ON THE FIRST SUNDAY OF JULY 1750, Jonathan Edwards preached his farewell sermon to the congregation in Northampton, Massachusetts ten days after they dismissed him as their pastor. Edwards had first been called to the church as assistant pastor in 1726 to work alongside his grandfather, the illustrious Solomon Stoddard. When Stoddard died in 1729, ending a pastorate that had lasted sixty years, Edwards succeeded him. Over the next twenty years, he led the church through two seasons of revival as it gained a reputation in the English-speaking world for the great work that God had done there. Despite this, there were growing tensions between Edwards and his congregation for several years. These strains finally reached a crisis point over the question of the basis upon which a person could be admitted to the Lord's Supper and become a member of the church in full standing. It was the culmination of this dispute, the Communion Controversy as it became known, that led to his removal.

Given the reasons for Edwards' dismissal, a good deal of scholarship, understandably, has focused on the reasons why this came about. Less attention, however, has been given to Edwards' theology of the Lord's Supper. Overall, the importance of his sacramental theology has often been dismissed and, in some accounts, the sacraments are scarcely, if at all, mentioned. This is surprising given the high estimation that Edwards gave to the Supper. One reason for this neglect is that it is part of a wider tendency in Edwards scholarship, following the influential Perry Miller, to relegate his ecclesiology to an area of little importance.[1] Another reason is that, apart from his writings on the Communion Controversy, Edwards offered no sustained treatment of the Supper. His primary means for exploring

[1]Miller, *Jonathan Edwards*, 31.

theological topics was the sermon. Here, as John Bombaro says, 'Edwards was able to string together several intimately and tangentially related theological, philosophical, biblical, and ethical themes, issues, concepts and present them with a sense of continuity and pervasive relevance.'[2] Yet, when it comes to the treatment of the Lord's Supper in his sermons some have detected a paucity of material. Robert Caldwell writes of the 'half dozen sacramental sermons, which he wrote specifically to be preached on the observance of the Lord's Supper, and which have never been published.'[3] While Elisha Cutter has claimed he only preached on communion in the fires of controversy.[4] William Danaher, in one of the few scholarly studies on Edwards and the Supper, has demonstrated, however, that he preached a considerable number of sermons on the subject over a twenty-seven year period, many of which are to be found in his unpublished writings.[5] Thanks to the work of the Jonathan Edwards Center at Yale University these sermons are now more easily accessible and widely available. This study will use this body of sermon material, along with his writings on the Communion Controversy and other texts in his corpus, to examine Edwards' views on the subject in more detail. While it must inevitably deal with the Communion Controversy, this is neither its only focus, nor is it the primary one. Rather, the Communion Controversy will be set in the context of Edwards' own understanding of the Lord's Supper. This will reveal, what Caldwell has described as, 'a more deeply sacramental view of the ordinance than has been recognized.'[6] It will also show that while his approach was within the bounds of orthodoxy 'his theology of the Supper pushed the envelope of Reformed thinking.'[7]

The reasons for Edwards' change of heart regarding admission to the Lord's Supper are not entirely clear. He later noted that he shifted his position as the result of his study of Scripture sometime in the early 1740s. What prompted him to undertake this line of enquiry is unknown. As several studies have noted there were external factors that played their part in his decision, alongside long-term unease over Stoddardeanism. How these

[2]Bombaro, "Dispositional Peculiarity", 139.

[3]Caldwell, *Communion*, 161, 162.

[4]Njoto, "The Lord's Supper", 29.

[5]Danaher, "By Sensible Signs", 262. There are more than thirty sacramental sermons, some of which were preached more than once.

[6]Caldwell, *Communion*, 162.

[7]McClymond and McDermott, *Theology of Jonathan Edwards*, 492.

various issues combined must remain a matter of some conjecture. It will become clear, however, in the course of this study that from the outset of his ministry, Edwards' theology of the Lord's Supper, as opposed to the practice in Northampton, was fully congruent with the theology that he later displayed in the defense he offered in *An Humble Inquiry* in 1749. It will become evident, therefore, that throughout his ministry as regards the Lord's Supper he must have, as Douglas Sweeney remarks, 'had to live with a fair amount of cognitive dissonance.'[8] As such, it seems that it may have been less a case of Edwards changing his mind, than finally following through on the practical implications of his own long term theological convictions.

Chapter one of this study will begin with a brief historical sketch looking at the issue of the Lord's Supper in its Reformation context. Particular attention will be given to the evolution of the sacrament in England and how this, in turn, shaped approaches to the subject in New England. This will be followed by some discussion of the New England controversies surrounding the Supper. While these debates pre-dated Edwards by several decades they, nonetheless, set the scene for his ministry and would ultimately frame the controversy in which he became embroiled.

Chapters two and three will consider how Edwards thought about the meaning of Lord's Supper. The focus will be upon his views of its celebration as an act of remembrance, a covenant seal, spiritual nourishment, communion with Christ and communion between believers. Chapter four will deal with the question of how a person should participate in the Lord's Supper, with specific attention given to the theme of self-examination. Chapter five will then consider the question of admission to the Supper and how this gave rise to the Communion Controversy. Here it will become clear that his defense of the idea that only those who could make a credible profession of faith should participate in the Supper involved the consistent application of views that are evident throughout his ministry.

The critical Yale edition of Edwards' works will be used throughout and will be cited in the established form of *WJE* for the published volumes and *WJEO* for the online volumes. Since many of the latter volumes have not been edited, I have engaged in some light editing for the sake of clarity.

[8] Sweeney, "The Church", 182.

Chapter One
Setting the Scene

IN THE MEDIEVAL WORLD, the sacramental system lay at the heart of the Western Church and society and the whole matter of salvation. The sacraments carried a person from the cradle to the grave, with the Mass playing a central role in this system. Its importance was such that, although there were seven sacraments, the term 'sacrament' became synonymous with the Mass. As Christopher Elwood states 'both theological definitions and popular religious practices placed the eucharist at the very center of religious life and underlined its status as the preeminent locus of divine power within the Christian's world of experience.'[1] In the Mass, through the miracle of transubstantiation, the communicant received the literal body of Christ in the bread and, with that, they received the pledge of salvation. Such was the power and importance of the Mass that it could even affect the afterlife, with masses being offered for the dead. By the eve of the Reformation, its celebration was a carefully choreographed ritual, suffused with mystery for all who watched the priest make this sacred offering, which culminated in the elevation of the host, as the bread, transformed into the body of Christ, was raised for all to see.

When the Reformers challenged the Roman Catholic Church's understanding of salvation by teaching that justification was by faith alone in the finished work of Christ, they struck at the heart of the sacramental system. Eventually, they reduced the number of sacraments from seven to two. The 1536 Geneva Catechism is representative of the Protestant view stating, 'Of [the sacraments] there are in the Christian Church only two which are insti-

[1]Elwood, *The Body Broken*, 4.

tuted by the authority of our Savior: Baptism and the Supper of our Lord; for what is held within the realm of the pope concerning seven sacraments, we condemn as fable and lie.'[2] Except for those on the radical wing, there was widespread agreement amongst the Reformers about baptism. As Michael Allen writes it 'was not a hot button issue in early Reformed confessions to the same degree as the Eucharist, largely because there were not as many concerns with Roman Catholic practice on this matter.'[3] Reaching agreement about the second sacrament, the Lord's Supper, proved to be problematic. While the Reformers were united, and often vehement, in their rejection of the Mass, and the associated idea of transubstantiation, they found it much more difficult to reach consensus on the nature and meaning of the Eucharist. This was, despite the fact, that as Heiko Oberman says, 'Only a few simple words were at issue, Christ's words instituting the Eucharist: "This is my body."'[4] The result was, as Elwood notes, 'The eucharist, the sacrament of the body and blood of Jesus Christ, was the focus of more theological controversy in the sixteenth century than any other item of Christian confession and practice.'[5]

What follows in the remainder of this chapter is not an attempt to trace the labyrinth ways of the Reformation debates on the Lord's Supper, which lies beyond the scope of this study.[6] Rather, it seeks to briefly highlight some of the key themes and debates that emerged as the Reformers sought a new understanding and consensus regarding the Supper. The chapter will then consider how the Supper came to be viewed during the English Reformation and, subsequently, in New England. It was these debates and the questions that they raised which shaped the tradition inherited by Jonathan Edwards.

The Lord's Supper in the European Reformation

In his 1520 work *Prelude on the Babylonian Captivity of the Church* Martin Luther rejected five of the seven sacraments of the Roman Catholic Church. He believed, however, that baptism and the Lord's Supper had been instituted by the Lord Jesus as signs of the grace and salvation that he had promised. Regarding the Supper, he denied the idea of transubstantiation, yet argued

[2]Cochrane, *Reformed Confessions,* 123.

[3]Allen, "Sacraments in the Reformed", 290.

[4]Oberman, *Luther,* 232.

[5]Elwood, *The Body Broken*, 3, 4.

[6]Anyone wishing to examine these debates in more detail might consult Wandel, *The Eucharist*.

that Christ was bodily present in the sacrament in a way that was ultimately mysterious. For Luther, the words of institution, *'Hoc est Corpus meum'*, must be understood literally, not figuratively, and he argued that Christ was present physically at the celebration of the Supper 'under' the bread. He stated,

> Christ gives his body to eat when he distributes the bread. On this we take our stand, and we also believe and teach that in the Supper we eat and take to ourselves Christ's body truly and physically. But how this takes place or how he is in the bread, we do not know and are not meant to know. We should believe God's Word without setting bound or measure to it. The bread we see with our eyes, but we hear with our ears that Christ's body is present.[7]

For Luther, it was only through Christ's physical presence in the Supper that those who participated by faith could be strengthened in their ongoing spiritual struggle.

During the early years of the Reformation, it became clear that Luther's understanding of the Supper was out of step with that of some of the other Reformers. His onetime colleague at Wittenberg, Andreas Karlstadt, and the Swiss Reformers Johannes Oecolampadius and Huldrych Zwingli, were among those who rejected his approach. At the core of their objections was the idea of the physical presence of Christ. They maintained that Christ could not both be exalted at the Father's right hand and, also, present in the bread in the manner that Luther affirmed. In response, Luther argued that since Christ was ubiquitous it was possible 'for the body of Christ to be not only in Heaven, but also at any place on earth, wherever God wants it to be.'[8] Consequently, he maintained that Christ must be physically present in the Supper. He resisted any attempts to separate Christ's physical and spiritual presence, or to spiritualize his presence at the Eucharist. Although, as Gordon Jenson observes, Luther may have 'suggested the idea of a *unio sacramentalis* (sacramental union) between the bread and wine and the body and blood of Christ, but he refused to try to explain how that happened.'[9]

In Zurich, Zwingli, who tended to deny any sense of indebtedness to Luther in shaping his Reformation principles, became the most outspoken

[7]Robinson, *The Annotated Luther*, 183.

[8]Leppin, "Martin Luther", 52.

[9]Jenson, "Luther and the Lord's Supper", 329.

opponent of his view of the Supper. In his 1528 work *On the Lord's Supper,* he identified, without naming Luther, as delusional those who maintained 'the bread is flesh and the wine blood, and that we partake of the flesh and blood really or essentially.'[10] He went as far as to state that this view was even less intelligible than the Mass. He argued that the Supper was simply a memorial meal, characterized by thanksgiving, which looked back to the historical event of the death of Christ. He wrote,

> our Lord Jesus Christ purposed to introduce a remembrance of his death, and his grace and redemption... a remembrance of that deliverance by which he redeemed the whole world, that we might never forget that for our sakes he exposed his body to the ignominy of death, and not merely that we might not forget in our hearts, but that we might publicly attest it with praise and thanksgiving, joining together for the greater magnifying and proclaiming of the matter in the eating and drinking of the sacrament of his sacred passion which is a representation of Christ's giving his body and shedding his blood for our sakes.[11]

Insofar as Christ was present, he was 'present not in the elements but, as the historical narrative is retold, he is present in his divinity in the community.'[12] In his memorialist approach Zwingli did acknowledge, however, the sanctity of the emblems, writing that 'The bread and the wine are materially unchanged, though in the context of the service the bread becomes sacred bread and acquires a dignity.'[13]

Such was the division among the Reformers over the Supper that Philip, the Landgrave of Hesse, in an attempt to stabilize the progress of the Reformation, invited Luther, Zwingli, and other leading figures to a conference to try to resolve their differences. The parties met at the Colloquy of Marburg in 1529 and, eventually, all agreed on fourteen articles drawn up by Luther. They could not agree, however, on the Lord's Supper, leading to a fifteenth article, drafted by Luther, which stated,

> we all believe and hold concerning the Supper of our dear Lord Jesus Christ that both kinds should be used according to the

[10] Bromiley, *Zwingli,* 186.

[11] Bromiley, *Zwingli*, 234.

[12] Spinks, *In Remembrance*, 278.

[13] Lane, "Calvin a Crypto-Zwinglian", 23.

> institution by Christ; [also that the mass is not a work with which one can secure grace for someone else, whether he is dead or alive;] also that the Sacrament of the Altar is a sacrament of the true body and blood of Jesus Christ and that the spiritual partaking of the same body and blood is especially necessary for every Christian. Similarly, that the use of the sacrament, like the word, has been given and ordained by God Almighty in order that weak consciences may thereby be excited to faith by the Holy Spirit. And although at this time, we have not reached an agreement as to whether the true body and blood of Christ are bodily present in the bread and wine, nevertheless, each side should show Christian love to the other side insofar as conscience will permit, and both sides should diligently pray to Almighty God that through his Spirit he might confirm us in the right understanding. Amen.[14]

After Marburg, despite their ongoing differences, Zwingli began to adopt a more nuanced memorialism stating that 'we believe Christ to be truly present in the Supper, indeed we do not believe that it is the Lord's Supper unless Christ is present.'[15] Although, it is debatable whether he had ever accepted the "bare" memorialism of which he was sometimes accused. Zwingli died in battle in 1531 but his influence remained strong among the Swiss Reformers, notably with his successor Heinrich Bullinger who both maintained Zwingli's views and developed them.

There was division not only between the Lutherans and the Reformed on the Supper but also among the Reformed churches. Initially, the Strasbourg Reformer Martin Bucer followed Zwingli's approach and adopted a view of the Supper as a memorial meal. By 1527, however, his approach had changed, and in the *Tetrapolitan Confession* of 1530 he rejected the idea 'that nothing save mere bread and mere wine is administered in our suppers.' Instead, he stated that in the Supper Christ 'deigns to give his true body and true blood to be truly eaten and drunk for the food and drink of souls, for their nourishment unto life eternal.'[16] Since Bucer, as Nicholas Thompson notes, was seeking a greater degree of rapprochement with the Lutherans

[14]Johnson, *Sacraments and Worship,* 234.

[15]Stephens, *Zwingli,* 105.

[16]Cochrane, *Reformed Confessions,* 75, 52.

'this statement avoided a more precise account of how Jesus's presence was tied either to the words and actions of the minister or to the elements.'[17]

Bucer's views exerted considerable influence on John Calvin during his exile in Strasbourg from 1538–541. Keith Mathison states that, upon his return to Geneva, Calvin began to largely follow Bucer, and 'his doctrine of the Supper was basically settled.'[18] Although, as Emidio Campi has remarked, his views might not be quite so easy to pin down. He points out 'Recent scholarship has demonstrated that Calvin's eucharistic thought cannot be approached as a finished and coherent theological product, but developed gradually and exhibits at different times Zwinglian (1536–1537), Lutheran and Bucerian (1537–1548), spiritualistic (1549–1560) and again Lutheran (1561–1562) impulses and leanings.'[19] Sue Rozeboom suggests that when considering Calvin's writings on the Supper there is a need to look at them as a whole since 'the aim of each of his works is unique, as the primary audience and occasioning circumstance of each differs.'[20] Despite the various developments in Calvin's views, it is evident that he rejected both the "bare" memorialism associated with Zwingli and, also, Luther's ideas concerning Christ's physical presence, although he was sympathetic to the emphases that each was trying to maintain.

By the final edition of the *Institutes* published in 1559 Calvin was able to state his belief that a sacrament is 'an external sign, by which the Lord seals on our consciences his promises of good-will toward us, in order to sustain the weakness of our faith.'[21] He argued for a close correlation between the symbol and what is signified, so that the symbol, and what is signified, are to be distinguished but not separated. Consequently, in the Supper, whilst there is no feeding upon the literal body and blood of Christ there is, nonetheless, a genuine feeding upon Christ. Nicholas Wolterstorff summarizes Calvin's view by stating that 'in the Eucharist, Christ's offering of his body and blood is both signified and effected, and the recipients' partaking of those is likewise both signified and effected. Christ is present in the sacrament in these two modes.'[22] Calvin admitted that how this feeding upon Christ

[17]Thompson, "Martin Bucer", 84.

[18]Mathison, "The Lord's Supper", 666.

[19]Campi, "Consensus Tigurinus", 7, 8. Others identify his eucharistic theology as going through five phases. For a summary see Bierma, *Font of Pardon,* 13, 14.

[20]Rozeboom, "The Lord's Supper", 143.

[21]Calvin, *Institutes,* IV. xiv.1.

[22]Wolterstorff, "John Calvin", 97.

occurred was a mystery. He concluded 'I rather feel than understand it.'[23] Or, as Lee Palmer Wandel comments, he 'did not try. . . to define the physics of the Supper.'[24]

While there was an element of mystery Calvin argued that the Supper involved 'spiritual eating' where Christ offered himself to the participants who fed upon him by faith. In doing so, they participated by faith, through the Holy Spirit, in the benefits won by Christ. The Supper was a means of spiritual nourishment for the believer where just as 'bread nourishes, sustains, and protects our bodily life, so the body of Christ is the only food to invigorate and keep alive the soul.'[25] It was an instrument of grace, but its instrumentality did not automatically convey grace. For Calvin, only those who are truly united to Christ benefit from participating in the Supper. There was no value in receiving it otherwise. He wrote 'I think it plain that there is no true and real eating by those who only eat the body of Christ sacramentally, seeing the body cannot be separated from its virtue.'[26] Furthermore, to participate in the meal in an unworthy manner brought with it spiritual danger as, this spiritual food, 'if given to a soul polluted with malice and wickedness, plunges it into greater ruin, not indeed by any defect in the food, but because to the "defiled and unbelieving is nothing pure" (Titus 1:15), however much it may be sanctified by the blessing of the Lord.'[27]

In Zurich Zwingli's successor, Bullinger, continued to uphold his mentor's memorialist view of the Supper. He did not, however, simply repeat it but modified it in keeping with his own theological development. In Bullinger's theology the Supper had 'soteriological significance.'[28] He saw it as closely related to the idea of covenant, which played a central role in his thought. Euler comments as 'symbols of the covenant of grace, the sacraments held for Bullinger more redemptive significance than they did for Zwingli. The water, bread, and wine were signs and could not convey grace themselves, but as symbols of grace, they could strengthen faith.'[29] Bullinger highlighted

[23]Calvin, *Institutes,* IV. xvii.32.

[24]Wandel, *The Eucharist,* 162.

[25]Calvin, *Institutes,* IV. xvii.3.

[26]Calvin, *Institutes,* IV. xvii.34.

[27]Calvin, *Institutes,* IV. xvii.40.

[28]Campi, "Consensus Tigurinus", 6.

[29]Euler, "Zwingli and Bullinger", 66.

the covenantal significance of meals writing 'At times, the most enduring covenants are consecrated by the breaking of bread.' Adding that 'Christ himself called the Supper a testament, "the new testament," which is "the remission of sins."[30] While his emphasis on covenant theology and the role of meals as a confirmatory sign added a new dimension to his theology of the Supper, he still retained a strong memorialist emphasis. In the First Helvetic Confession of 1536 Bullinger denied that memorialism meant that their churches attached little value to the Supper, rather 'they bear witness to things that have happened. . . And by means of a singular resemblance to the things they signify, they shed a great and glorious light upon sacred and divine matters.'[31]

In the 1540s against a background of political and ecclesiastical turbulence, Bullinger and Calvin engaged in a largely private dialogue seeking agreement on the Supper. The outcome of this discussion was the 1549 *Consensus Tigurinus*. The *Consensus* represented a compromise between the two Reformers. The document upheld the language of Zwingli and Bullinger, that the Supper was a sign and, it also reflected Calvin's view that there was correspondence between the sign and the spiritual reality and gifts communicated to the believer through the Holy Spirit. As Peter Stephens comments 'It could be described as a Calvinian view expressed within the constraints imposed by Bullinger's theology or Bullinger's view stretched to embrace Calvin's.'[32] It made clear, however, that a person could receive the bread and the wine without any inherent spiritual benefit. Alongside this, the document denied the idea of the real presence as conceived by both the Catholics and the Lutherans.

Naturally, the *Consensus* did not please the Lutherans, who saw Calvin as capitulating to the memorialism of Zurich, but it did improve the relationship between Zurich and Geneva and eventually found a degree of consent from the other Swiss churches. Yet, as Mathison points out, it represented 'the theology of neither Bullinger nor Calvin completely. Each made concessions in order to produce a formulation both sides could sign.'[33] As a result, Calvin 'would defend the *Consensus* by interpreting it along the lines of his own doctrine of the Supper.'[34] In 1559 he wrote,

[30] Baker, "Heinrich Bullinger", 366, footnote 34.

[31] Cochrane, *Reformed Confessions*, 109.

[32] Quoted in Euler, "Zwingli and Bullinger", 68.

[33] Mathison, "The Lord's Supper", 668.

[34] Mathison, "The Lord's Supper", 669.

> We believe, as has been said, that in the Lord's Supper, as well as in baptism, God gives us really and in fact that which he there sets forth to us; and that consequently with these signs is given the true possession and enjoyment of that which they present to us. And thus all who bring a pure faith, like a vessel, to the sacred table of Christ, receive truly that of which it is a sign; for the body and the blood of Jesus Christ give food and drink to the soul, no less than bread and wine nourish the body.[35]

Bullinger was quite sanguine about the *Consensus* arguing 'that it has borne fruit splendidly.'[36] His later sacramental theology revealed his indebtedness to Calvin. The Second Helvetic Confession, which he authored in 1562 and revised in 1564, stated,

> Therefore the faithful receive what is given by the ministers of the Lord, and they eat the bread of the Lord and drink of the Lord's cup. At the same time by the work of Christ through the Holy Spirit they also inwardly receive the flesh and blood of the Lord, and are thereby nourished unto life eternal. For the flesh and blood of Christ is the true food and drink unto eternal life.[37]

As Gerald Bray has written 'One way or another, the Consensus Tigurinus became foundational to the Reformed understanding of the Lord's Supper.'[38] Indeed, as Campi points out, with the publication of Bullinger's *Decades* and the final edition of the *Institutes* the ideas of both authors were widely disseminated throughout Europe.[39]

Surveying developments in Europe it becomes clear that there was not a single Reformed view of the Lord's Supper. While the terms 'Calvinism' and 'Reformed' are often used interchangeably, it is important not to assume that this necessarily implies that Calvin was the single fountainhead of the Reformed tradition. This is clearly not the case concerning the Lord's Supper where, as Mathison comments, 'The sixteenth-century Reformed Confessions reflect the range of views among theologians of that time.'[40]

[35] Quoted in Spinks, *In Remembrance*, 290.

[36] Quoted in Campi, "Consensus Tigurinus", 21.

[37] Cochrane, *Reformed Confessions*, 284.

[38] Bray, *God Has Spoken*, 880.

[39] Campi, "Consensus Tigurinus", 24.

[40] Mathison, "The Lord's Supper", 670.

Furthermore, as Richard Muller has pointed out we need to take care when approaching a range of subjects, including the Lord's Supper, not to think that 'Calvin proposed a highly unique doctrine.'[41] Or that he bequeathed a tradition that others in the Reformed tradition believed they were obliged to uphold. Rather, as Graeme Murdock has observed, the international Reformed movement was part of a 'religious tradition which, despite its debt to John Calvin, was always very much more than a product of his life and work in Geneva.'[42] This was something that Edwards recognized when wrote, 'I should not take it at all amiss, to be called a Calvinist, for distinction's sake: though I utterly disclaim a dependence on Calvin, or believing the doctrines which I hold, because he believed and taught them; and cannot justly be charged with believing in everything just as he taught.'[43]

It is important to bear this in mind when considering the Lord's Supper in the context of the English Reformation. While it was influenced by the Reformation in Europe, and some of its proponents were dubbed 'Calvinists', it did not draw upon Calvin as its single source of inspiration. Stephen Mayor rather overstates the matter when he writes that the Puritans were 'in general satisfied that Calvin had said the last word on the theology even if not on the liturgy of the Eucharist.'[44] For example, as the Presbyterian Richard Rogers noted, the Lord's Supper had been largely dealt with not only by Calvin but also by Beza and Peter Martyr.[45] As Rogers' comment show, English authors drew upon an eclectic group of theologians whose ideas they then developed in a way that reflected the issues that arose in their own context. Often, these were not the concerns that had troubled the early European Reformers.

The Lord's Supper in the English Reformation

The Reformation in England was initially different in character from that in continental Europe. This was because it was initially political, rather than religious, having been stimulated by King Henry VIII's divorce, his so-called 'great matter'. For this reason, Henry, while rejecting the authority of the Pope, nonetheless, remained Catholic in his theology and was antithetical to

[41]Muller, *Calvin and the Reformed,* 52.

[42]Murdock, *Beyond Calvin,* 5.

[43]*WJE* 1:131.

[44]Mayor, *The Lord's Supper*, 26.

[45]Holifield, *The Covenant Sealed*, 40.

Protestantism. Behind the scenes, several key figures, notably Thomas Cranmer who became the Archbishop of Canterbury in 1533, cautiously sought to introduce a measure of reform. At this time the English Reformation was largely shaped by Luther. As Carl Trueman writes, 'it is simply impossible to understand the nature of English Reformation thought without reference to the theology of Martin Luther. Indeed, as the English Reformers moved beyond Humanism, it was to Wittenberg that they turned for inspiration.'[46]

When Henry was succeeded by his young son Edward VI there was a move towards greater reform which, again, was guided by Cranmer. As this reform was gradually introduced it was resisted by conservatives in the Church and criticized by the more reform minded. The result was that Cranmer's 1549 *Prayer Book* was a compromise document. In terms of the Lord's Supper, it sought to placate Protestants by removing the more offensive elements of the Mass while retaining other aspects, such as the altar, in an attempt to satisfy conservatives. By the introduction of the Act of Uniformity in 1552, the *Prayer Book* had been revised along more thoroughly Protestant lines, reflecting Cranmer's mature Eucharistic thought.

Like the English Reformation itself, Cranmer's ideas about the Supper evolved over several years. By the 1550s he was arguing for the spiritual presence of Christ at its celebration. Those who participated in the Supper fed upon Christ in a spiritual way, by receiving the benefits of Christ's work on the cross and being nurtured in their faith. In this way, as Diarmaid MacCulloch notes, 'God works *by* his sacraments *in* those who rightly receive them.'[47] In Cranmer's view, the emphasis was less upon grace being conveyed in the Supper, than upon the recipient exercising faith in the reality that lay behind the symbol. As he wrote in *A Defence of the True and Catholic Doctrine of the Sacrament of the Body and Blood of our Saviour Christ* 'figuratively [Christ] is in the bread and wine, and spiritually he is in them that worthily eat and drink the bread and wine; but really, carnally, and corporally he is only in heaven from whence he shall come to judge the quick and dead.'[48] As Gordon Pruett comments for Cranmer 'on the one hand faith is necessary for the real participation in Christ, and on the other the activity of the Holy Spirit promises the presence of the body and blood through divine grace.'[49] This emphasis on the importance of the right

[46]Trueman, *Luther's Legacy,* 54.

[47]MacCulloch, *Thomas Cranmer,* 614.

[48]Cranmer, *A Defence,* 308.

[49]Pruett, "A Protestant Doctrine", 165.

reception of the Supper was something that became deeply ingrained in the English church.

The changes introduced by Cranmer in 1552 were short-lived as Edward died the following year and was replaced by his half-sister Mary, during whose rule England once more reverted to Catholicism. At the end of Mary's reign, in 1558, the realm again became Protestant under her half-sister Elizabeth. With the accession of Elizabeth, England adopted the form of Protestantism that was bequeathed by the martyred Cranmer. This was a disappointment to many Protestants who had hoped for a more thorough-going reform of the Church of England. For some of those who advocated further reform their ideas about the nature of the church had been shaped during their exile under Mary, which they spent in centers of the Reformation, such as Geneva and Zurich. Their dissatisfaction with the Elizabethan settlement and desire for ongoing reform led to them being dubbed 'Precisionists' and, more widely, 'Puritans.' The Puritans were a diverse group, with some prepared to largely accept the Church of England in its existing form while hoping for future reform; others advocated a throughgoing Presbyterian church. Others were frustrated by the failure of the Church to implement change and sought more radical solutions which eventually led to the rise of Separatism. Despite this diversity the lack of dispute over the nature of the Lord's Supper indicates that there was a good deal of consensus on the subject among all shades of Puritanism. As James Turrell has observed, 'While puritans dissented from several liturgical practices in the prayer book's communion rite, and some rejected the use of a set form of prayer at all, they did not differ sharply from conformist eucharistic theology.'[50]

The importance of the right reception of the Supper was an idea that, in English theology went back to Cranmer. Some Puritans, following in this vein, came to lay particular emphasis on this and, consequently, they highlighted the need to prepare properly to participate in the sacrament. The prominence given to preparation owed much to William Perkins, who was one of the key architects of English Reformed theology. Perkins defined a sacrament as 'A sign to represent, a seal to confirm, an instrument to convey Christ and all His Benefits to them that do believe in Him.'[51] The Lord's Supper should be conducted 'according to the custom of the Church

[50]Turrell, "Anglican Theologies", 149.

[51]Perkins, *Foundation of Christian Religion,* 505.

whereof we are members... without addition, detraction, or change.'[52] In its celebration, he maintained that, 'The former covenant solemnly ratified in baptism, is renewed in the Lord's Supper, between the Lord Himself, and the receiver.'[53] He also emphasized the need for those participating in the Supper to have experienced regeneration, stating that it was to be received by 'Everyone that has been baptized and after his baptism has truly believed in Christ and has repented of his sins from his heart.' Perkins then posed, a seemingly unusual question, 'What shall a true receiver feel in himself after the receiving of the Sacrament?'[54] He answered that the recipient should 'feel in himself the increase of his faith in Christ, the increase of sanctification, a greater measure of dying to sin, a greater care to live in newness of life.' Anyone who did not enjoy such an experience after receiving the Supper should question if they had ever truly come to know Christ and seek the means to come to true faith and repentance.[55] The Supper ought to be experimental and only those who were worthy recipients could expect to enjoy its benefits. His concern for the worthy reception of the sacrament reflects, what Theodore Bozeman calls, Perkins' emphasis on 'exacting inward analysis.'[56]

In his work, *A Golden Chain* Perkins stated that while in the Supper Christ might be offered to all, including hypocrites, it was only given 'to the faithful for the daily increase of their faith, and repentance.'[57] In eating and drinking, a person sealed 'his application of Christ by faith, that the feeling of his true union and communion with Christ may daily be increased.'[58] He rejected transubstantiation and, what opponents of Lutheranism termed, consubstantiation since, if 'Christ's body were eaten corporally, then should the wicked as well as the faithful be partakers of the flesh of Christ; but to eat His flesh, is to believe in Him, and to have eternal life.'[59] In light of this, Perkins stressed the importance of preparation in coming to the Supper, since this was 'a medicine to the diseased and languishing soul; and therefore

[52]Perkins, *A Reformed Catholic,* 508.

[53]Perkins, *Foundation of Christian Religion,* 507.

[54]Perkins, *Foundation of Christian Religion,* 507.

[55]Perkins, *Foundation of Christian Religion,* 507.

[56]Quoted in Patterson, *William Perkins,* 61.

[57]Perkins, *A Golden Chain,* 167.

[58]Perkins, *A Golden Chain,* 167.

[59]Perkins, *A Golden Chain,* 168.

men must as well seek to purify and heal their hearts in it as to bring pure and sound hearts unto it.'[60] Perkins' views on the Supper reflected the strain in English Reformed thought that emphasized the subjective element of participation in the Lord's Supper rather than its instrumentality. It also pointed towards the idea of the mutual sealing of the covenant that occurred in the Supper. Perkins stated that 'The means are God's covenant and the seal thereof. . . This covenant consists of two parts: God's promise to man; man's promise to God.'[61] The idea of mutual sealing became an important dimension of how the Supper was understood in both England and New England.

By the late Elizabethan era it was becoming obvious to some Puritans that their hope for further reform of the Church had stalled. Some began to advocate, in the words of Robert Browne's famous treatise of 1582, *Reformation without Tarying for Anie.* While some continued to be hopeful of further reform, and others made their peace with the Church of England, groups of Separatists now began to emerge. With the appearance of these groups, questions about the meaning of the Lord's Supper became less important than questions about participation in the Lord's Supper. The emphasis among the Separatists was on the purity of the church, which had great implications for the administration of the sacraments. Some of them believed that it was not acceptable to receive the Supper in the Church of England, which they had come to regard as an apostate church. They argued that only a pure church, made up of professing believers, could properly administer the sacraments. As one early Separatist, John Greenwood, stated 'if you have no true church, you have no true sacraments.'[62] There was a particular focus among these groups on the corporate dimension of the Supper as a covenant seal given to the church. As Mayor states their 'conception of the Lord's Supper as a mark of belonging to the Church meant that no one inside the Church should be excluded from Communion.'[63] If no one inside the church should be excluded from communion, then the great question became, who belonged inside the church?

The manner in which the Lord's Supper came to be celebrated amongst such Dissenters created a strange paradox where it was held in high regard, yet it came to be celebrated less frequently. Arnold Hunt's remarks about

[60] Perkins, *A Golden Chain*, 169.

[61] Perkins, *A Golden Chain*, 65.

[62] Greenwood, *Writings of John Greenwood*, 26.

[63] Mayor, *The Lord's Supper*, 41.

communion in the Church of England are equally applicable to Dissenters. He notes that ministers who 'set their standards too high in their efforts to encourage their flocks to prepare more carefully for receiving the sacrament, ended up discouraging them receiving it at all. Protestant teaching may have succeeded too well, reinforcing popular respect for the sacrament in a way that its authors neither intended nor desired, and that proved pastorally self-defeating.[64]

Separatists remained largely on the fringes of the English ecclesiastical scene until the Civil War which created two decades of uncertainty in English life and the proliferation of dissenting movements. During the Civil War, there was an attempt to reconstruct the Church of England along more Reformed lines. This led to the calling of the Westminster Assembly, which was first convened in 1643. The Assembly set about revising the Thirty-Nine Articles and, in doing so, produced the Westminster Standards[65] which are often viewed as the high watermark of Puritan theology. It is perhaps then ironic that, as B.A. Gerrish writes, 'the Westminster Confession's teaching on the sacraments (1647) is not so plainly Calvinistic as the teaching of the Anglican catechism. . . The Calvinistic intention of their teaching has to be gleaned from incidental phrases that presuppose the instrumental view.'[66] In fact, as Gerrish points out, there are some inconsistencies in the Standards in terms of their view of the Supper. This observation helps to support his conclusion that 'The judgement that Calvin's eucharistic teaching "must be regarded as the orthodox Reformed doctrine" oversimplifies the evidence.'[67] With the restoration of the monarchy in 1660 the Church of England again embraced the Thirty-Nine Articles while Presbyterian Dissenters held to the Westminster Standards, or in the case of Congregationalists and Baptists variations of the Confession.

The Lord's Supper in New England

For some Dissenters disillusionment with the Church of England, and persecution by it, led them into exile. At first, they traveled to the Netherlands,

[64]Hunt, "The Lord's Supper", 83.

[65]The Westminster Standards include the Westminster Confession of Faith, the Westminster Shorter Catechism, the Westminster Larger Catechism, the Directory of Public Worship, and the Form of Church Government.

[66]Gerrish, *The Old Protestantism,* 126.

[67]Gerrish, *The Old Protestantism,* 128.

and later to the North American colonies. It was upon settling in the latter that their vision of the church and its practices reached its fullest expression. It was here too that, while they coalesced around a set of ideals, they discovered many of the difficulties in implementing them.

Once in New England Dissenters 'gradually evolved a Congregational form of church government and sought a sacramental practice consonant with that of the primitive church of the New Testament.'[68] In the development of their ecclesiology they were especially indebted to William Ames who was Perkins' 'protégé'.[69] Ames had influenced the English community in the Netherlands and, it was hoped, that once the colonists were established in New England he would join them, but he died before this was possible. Despite this 'his books and reputation preceded him and were deeply appreciated.'[70] As John Eusden has written, 'in early American theological and intellectual history, William Ames was without peer'[71] and his work *The Marrow of Theology* became the standard theological textbook at Harvard.[72] The profound impact of Ames' theology on New England means that he is sometimes considered to be the father of the 'New England Way'. In terms of his ecclesiology, he viewed the church as a 'visible congregation', a covenanted community, consisting of 'a society of believers joined together by a special bond among themselves, for the constant exercise of the communion of Saints among themselves.'[73] As such Ames, unlike Calvin, emphasized the visibility of the invisible church. Furthermore, Spinks remarks that his sacramental theology was 'more akin to Bullinger and Laski than Calvin and Beza.'[74] Like Perkins, his emphasis was less upon the presence of Christ at the Supper, than upon Christ's presence in the believer.

Despite his view of the church as a visible congregation, Ames did not discount the place of children within it. He maintained that the 'children of those believers who are in the Church are also to be accounted as members of the Church... For they are partakers of the same covenant, and of the same

[68]Holifield, "Sacramental Theology in America", 383.

[69]Vliet, *Rise of Reformed System,* 6.

[70]Vliet, *Rise of Reformed System,* xv.

[71]Ames, *The Marrow of Theology*, 11.

[72]'Ames's work was not only extraordinarily influential in early New England theology, but also belonged to Edwards's core works of study at Yale College and thereafter. 'Neele, *Before Jonathan Edwards*, 164.

[73]Ames, *The Marrow of Theology,* 179.

[74]Spinks, *In Remembrance*, 301.

profession with their parents.'[75] The children of believers could, therefore, be presented for baptism since, he argued, 'The primary end of a Sacrament is to seal the Covenant.'[76] Children did not, however, have an automatic right to the Lord's Supper as 'infants are not such mature members of the Church that they can exercise acts of communion, or be admitted to partake of all its privileges, unless there first appears an increase of Faith.'[77] The Lord's Supper was 'only to be administered to those who are visibly capable of nourishment and growth in the Church; and so it is not to be administered to Infants, but only to those who are of age.'[78] As he wrote in *Conscience with the Power and Cases Thereof* 'the knowledge of the principal grounds of religion, necessary to salvation, is necessary also to the discerning of the sacrament.'[79] Only those who had truly undergone a work of salvation should participate in the Supper. This preempted the discussion in New England of who should be admitted to Lord's Table.

In New England 'the chief helmsman'[80] of the ecclesiastical system that developed was John Cotton, who had studied under Ames. In his fullest expression of polity, *The Way of Congregational Churches Cleared*, he stated that it was from Ames that he 'received light out of the word, for the matter of the visible church to be visible saints.'[81] To maintain the purity of the church, Cotton argued, it was necessary that the church was 'satisfied in the sincerity of the regeneration of such who are to be received'[82] into full communicant membership. This gave rise to the 'conversion narrative' by which those seeking membership demonstrated, by recounting their conversion before the church, the likelihood that they were truly the children of God. While the idea of the morphology of conversion had a long pedigree among Puritans, going back to Perkins and Richard Rogers, the idea of recounting one's steps through this process to gain entrance to the church went beyond what either the English Puritans or the Reformed churches in Europe required. As Brooks Holifield has remarked, 'The New England ideal of pure churches, composed

[75]Ames, *The Marrow of Theology,* 179, 180.

[76]Ames, *The Marrow of Theology,* 198, 199.

[77]Ames, *The Marrow of Theology,* 180.

[78]Ames, *The Marrow of Theology,* 212.

[79]Ames, *Conscience,* Book IV, 84.

[80]Ziff, *John Cotton,* 5.

[81]Ziff, *John Cotton*, 189.

[82]Quoted in Pettit, *The Heart Prepared*, 134.

of members who had been reborn of the Spirit and bound together by explicit covenants, stood in tension with historic conceptions of sacramental practice.'[83]

The implementation of this ideal was also fraught with difficulties since it was not agreed what the exact pattern of the work of the Holy Spirit in the life of an individual looked like. As a result, it gave rise to the preparationism debate that dominated New England church life throughout the century. This, as Janice Knight points out, led to disagreements over 'the order of salvation, the relationship between preparation and assurance, God's complete prevenience and the efficacy of human cooperation, and the nature of God's covenantal promises.'[84] It also tended to have a deadening effect upon the spiritual vitality that it was supposed to foster, where those who related their experience, and those who listened, became less concerned with a true account of conversion than with one which accorded with the accepted formula and phraseology. Furthermore, while this matter had implications for church membership, it also had civic implications since, in New England, only those who were church members could become freemen and enjoy all the political privileges of the Commonwealth. This ensured the continuation of a society in which church and state, while officially separated, were inextricably linked.

By the middle of the seventeenth century, the weaknesses of this system began to emerge. The spiritual fervor that had marked the first generation of settlers had abated and, as a result, few people presented themselves for membership. This meant that, in turn, they could not present their children for baptism. It seemed to many observers that the cohesion of church and society that had marked the life of the early settlers was now beginning to break down. Against this background, a synod met in 1662 to clarify an earlier ruling of 1657 on suitable candidates for baptism. The 1662 synod confirmed that baptized children obtained a permanent right of membership in the church and that upon reaching maturity they had a right to offer their children for baptism by 'owning' the covenant' i.e., they did not live scandalous lives and professed the doctrines of the faith. While the synod introduced a broader view of church membership, it nonetheless reaffirmed that the privileges of the Lord's Supper and voting were still to be reserved for those who could account for a true work of God's grace in their lives. Critics dubbed the ruling the 'Half-way Covenant.' As Edmund Morgan has

[83]Holifield, *The Covenant Sealed*, 140.

[84]Knight, *Orthodoxies in Massachusetts*, 20.

commented it 'brought into the open the difficulties that had been lurking in the Puritan conception of church membership from the beginning.'[85]

While the decision of the synod may have broadened the basis for church membership it did not increase the number of conversions or those seeking full communicant membership of the churches. David Hall has written 'almost every congregation contained a clump of persons who attended regularly, were deemed Christians in how they behaved, had their children baptized (early or late), but who never came forward to describe themselves as converted.'[86] This was due, in part, to the emphasis on true conversion for participants and the dread of eating and drinking unworthily which 'produced the gravest anxiety among many potential communicants'[87] whose experience did not conform to the preparationist pattern. Once again, paradoxically, a high view of the Supper made 'the sacraments seem irrelevant to the majority of the population and the greater part of the congregations.'[88]

This was an issue of some unease for the Northampton pastor, Solomon Stoddard, who was an early proponent of the 'Half-way Covenant' and who was concerned equally about both the neglect and profanation of the Supper. He had a great pastoral burden and, as Holifield notes, he was motivated by 'the desire of families to ensure that their children would receive the benefits of the covenant. The impulse to preserve the wellbeing of the family and to care for children informed innovation.'[89] He was also concerned about the decreasing influence of the church in New England society which he attributed, in part, to its founders and their 'closed, inward-looking quest for a pure body of saints.'[90] His alternative 'vision of church and state if implemented, was intended to conquer America for God and advance the world towards the inevitable victory of righteousness.'[91] In a move towards an enlarged vision of the church, Stoddard persuaded the synod that met at Westfield in 1679 to drop the requirement of a conversion narrative for new communicants, and to replace it with a profession of faith and repentance. As he later recorded 'they blotted out that clause of Making a Relation of the

[85]Morgan, *Visible Saints,* 138.

[86]Hall, "New England, 1660–1730", 148.

[87]Davies, *American Puritans,* 169.

[88]Davies, *American Puritans,* 159.

[89]Holifield, *The Covenant Sealed,* 384.

[90]Lucas, "Death of the Prophet", 78.

[91]Lucas, "Death of the Prophet", 77.

work of God's Spirit, and put in the room of it the Making a Profession of Faith and Repentance.'[92]

Having removed this bar to communion Stoddard by 1690 was suggesting a radical and innovative approach to the Supper. In a sermon based on Galatians 3:1, he stated 'As the Passover of old was, the Lords Supper now is appointed for conversion.'[93] As David McDowell writes, 'Opening communion to all visible saints, whether proven regenerate or not, was Stoddard's evangelical method of casting the gospel net as wide as possible, thus preparing as many souls as possible to come into contact with the grace of God.'[94] By allowing all such 'visible saints' to participate in the Supper, Stoddard believed that many more could be brought to faith, the church enlarged and its influence extended.

Stoddard met with a good deal of opposition noting 'Men are wont to make a great Noise that we are bringing in Innovations, and depart from the Old Ways.'[95] Despite the accusation of apparent innovation, the idea of the Supper as a converting ordinance was not entirely new. Holifield points out that at the Westminster Assembly William Prynne, whose views had shifted from Presbyterian to Erastian, 'introduced into the debate a definition of a sacrament as a "converting ordinance."'[96] He did so believing that 'common admission to the sacrament, in a Church carefully administered by government officials who would ensure that communicants lead lives of decency and decorum, was the only means to oversee and protect the moral welfare of England.'[97] As Paul Lucas states, 'For Prynne, and for others, the converting ordinances unleashed spiritual power vital in winning souls and bringing about moral reform.'[98] Prynne rejected the idea that only the regenerate should be admitted to the Supper, and argued that any who had not been excommunicated and who accepted Christian doctrine should be permitted to celebrate it. It was, he thought, no more unacceptable for sincere persons to attend communion than it was for them to attend the

[92]Davis and Jeske, "Stoddard's 'Arguments'", 78.

[93]Quoted in McDowell, *Half-Way Covenant*, 59. According to Davis 'There is no evidence before the Galatians sermon... to indicate that Stoddard was inclined to such a view.' Davis, "Solomon Stoddard's Sermon", 205, footnote 1.

[94]McDowell, *Half-Way Covenant*, 61.

[95]Quoted in Hall, *Last American Puritan*, 319.

[96]Holifield, *The Covenant Sealed*, 113.

[97]Holifield, *The Covenant Sealed*, 111.

[98]Lucas, "Death of the Prophet", 76.

preaching of the word, since Christ was present in both. Despite being rejected at Westminster his views 'informed English and American sacramental discussion for well over a century.'[99]

Prynne who was Stoddard's 'mentor'[100] had a vision of the moral reformation of society, the place of the church in that society, and the function of the Supper as a converting ordinance. These views were all shared by Stoddard who, in 1700, went into print about the Supper in his work *The Doctrine of Instituted Churches: Explained and Proved from the Word of God.* Many of the arguments he put forward echoed those of Prynne. Stoddard having moved away from the idea that a relation of religious experience was necessary for admission to the sacrament, argued that 'a Profession of the faith joyned with a good Conversation, is a sufficient ground for Charity'[101] in this matter. In the New Testament such people, he argued, were regarded as 'Visible Saints' and their profession of faith was the basis for admission to the church, which made 'no distinction of the Adult Members of the Church, into Communicants and Non-Communicants.'[102] He did not see this as diminishing the importance of the Supper and he reminded those who neglected it that God commanded all who were qualified to participate in the sacrament to do so. If they did not obey this commandment, then it was a sin. He further argued that no one should be barred from the Lord's Supper on the grounds of 'not giving the highest evidence of sincerity' because there had never been 'any such Law in the Church of God.'[103]

Stoddard's standards of admission were closer to those of old England and once more he put baptism and the Supper on a par with each other. Indeed, he saw the Lord's Supper as being equal to the other means that God employed in bringing people to faith. He stated that those who knew themselves to still be in a natural condition 'may and ought to come' to the Supper since 'this Ordinance is instituted for all the Adult Members of the Church who are not scandalous.'[104] He continued 'as no Man may neglect Prayer, or hearing the Word, because he cannot do it in Faith, so

[99]Holifield, *The Covenant Sealed.* 113.

[100]Lucas, "Death of the Prophet", 74.

[101]Stoddard, *Instituted Churches,* 19.

[102]Stoddard, *Instituted Churches,* 19.

[103]Stoddard, *Instituted Churches,* 20.

[104]Stoddard, *Instituted Churches,* 21.

he may not neglect the Lord's Supper.'[105] Since all ordinances including baptism, preaching, and prayer were appointed for regeneration it would, therefore, 'be strange if the Lord's Supper alone should not be appointed for that end.'[106] As he would later argue, those who thought otherwise were in danger of making 'an idol of the Lord's Supper.'[107]

While some saw his views as unsettling, the idea of equating word and the sacrament was not innovative. For example, Calvin, following Augustine, had viewed the sacraments as 'a visible word.'[108] Perkins argued that the sacraments and preaching 'are one in substance'[109] with the difference being that in one of them God is heard and in the other seen. As the Presbyterian leaning Thomas Watson had written in the seventeenth century, 'A sacrament is a visible sermon. And herein the sacrament excels the Word preached. The Word is a trumpet to proclaim Christ. The sacrament is a glass to represent Him.' Consequently, as Watson continued, 'when we see Christ broken in the bread and, as it were, crucified before us, this more affects our hearts than the "bare" preaching of the Word.'[110] Stoddard was simply taking this understanding to what he considered to be its logical conclusion.

Stoddard was careful, however, to ensure that his argument was not taken as an endorsement of open communion. He wrote 'The Lord's Supper is Instituted to be a means of Regeneration, it is not appointed for the converting of men to the Christian Religion, for only such as are Converted may partake of it; but it is not only for the strengthening of Saints but a means also to work saving Regeneration.'[111] The Supper, he continued, 'is a particular Invitation to sinners, to come to Christ for Pardon, here is an affecting Representation of the Virtue of Christ's sufferings, here is a Seal whereby the Truth of the Gospel is confirmed, all of which are very proper to draw sinners to Christ.'[112] At the same time, he warned that those who took the Supper, and who were not saints, were guilty of profaning it. He

[105] Stoddard, *Instituted Churches,* 21.

[106] Stoddard, *Instituted Churches,* 22.

[107] Stoddard, *Appeal to the Learned,* 53.

[108] Calvin, *Institutes,* IV. xiv.6.

[109] Quoted in Patterson, *William Perkins*, 104.

[110] Watson, *The Holy Eucharist,* 2, 3.

[111] Stoddard, *Instituted Churches*, 22.

[112] Stoddard, *Instituted Churches,* 22.

maintained that 'that the Lords Supper is a Converting Ordinance, only for Church Members.'[113]

As Hall points out, 'some, possibly a significant percentage, resisted acting on Stoddard's interpretation of the Lord's Supper.'[114] Consequently, it was not until 1710 that his own congregation voted to adopt his controversial ideas. More widely, his ideas were not well-received, and he was strongly opposed by many in New England, including such prominent figures as the Mathers and Edward Taylor. Yet, by the 1720s his views had weathered the storm, and garnered favor among a younger generation of ministers who 'agreed with him that exclusionary policies regarding baptism and the Lord's Supper hindered the progress of evangelism.'[115] It appears, however, that it was only in Northampton that his principles on the Supper were adopted and put into practice. Furthermore, the new policy had little effect, it seems, in encouraging the townspeople to participate in the sacrament. In Northampton, as Rhys Bezzant observes, 'the challenge was not overreliance on the sacraments, but nominal appreciation by some of their benefits, and refusal by others to take the Supper at all.'[116]

By 1726, when his grandson Jonathan Edwards arrived at Northampton as his assistant, Stoddard's practice regarding the Lord's Supper was well-established. Edwards, however, had grown up under the ministry of his father Timothy, who had continued the more traditional approach of requiring a conversion narrative for admission to the Supper. Consequently, Edwards' disciple and biographer Samuel Hopkins remarked that upon his arrival at Northampton he had some scruples about Stoddard's practice, and this continued for some time. Although, as Hopkins added, he 'did not receive such a degree of conviction, that the admitting of persons into the church, who made no pretense to real godliness was wrong as to prevent his practicing upon it with good conscience, for some years.'[117] Thomas Schafer has concluded that at this time 'he was, on the whole, comfortable with Stoddard's ecclesiology'[118] while John Jamieson writes that he 'was able to conform to established practice without difficulty for almost two decades

[113]Stoddard, *Instituted Churches* 26.

[114]Editor's Introduction, *WJE* 12:44.

[115]Editor's Introduction, *WJE* 12:42.

[116]Bezzant, "Ecclesiology and Sacraments", 268.

[117]Hopkins, *Life and Character,* 61.

[118]Editor's Introduction, *WJE* 13:26.

after Stoddard's death.'[119] Bezzant, perhaps, comes closest to Edwards' initial frame of mind when he states that he had to 'decide in his earliest years how to appropriate the gift of his New England ecclesiological heritage and how to nail his own theological colors to the mast without damaging or disowning thanklessly the patrimony preserved for him.'[120]

After Stoddard's death, when he assumed the pastorate in full, Edwards began in his private writings to challenge some of his grandfather's views.[121] Kenneth Minkema writes,

> in his sermons and private notes during this period, Edwards was distancing himself from Stoddard's views on conversion and the sacraments. Edwards suspected that the "dullness" or unresponsiveness of a significant portion of his congregation to the preaching of the new birth was attributable to their willingness to rely on a past identifiable experience, or a "supposed" day of grace, and on their status as unconverted full members.'[122]

While there was little direct public utterance in this regard, he wrote several entries in the *Miscellanies* in 1728 about church membership and he again took up the matter in 1730.[123] Edwards was pulling at a thread in Stoddardeanism which, by the 1740s, would lead in his mind to the unraveling of the entire system and, as a consequence, his dismissal from the Northampton congregation when his views became public.

Initially, Edwards may have reconciled himself to the practice of Stoddard's ecclesiology, and while the Communion Controversy lay several years in the future, the seeds of his views may be seen in his theology of the Lord's Supper which is reflected in his sermons and other writings. Here it becomes apparent that Edwards did not so much change his mind regarding the Lord's Supper, as finally put into practice his own long-term convictions. As he acknowledged in a letter to John Erskine in Scotland in May 1749, as the Communion Controversy was at its height, 'I formerly conformed to his practice, but I have had difficulties with respect to it, which have been long increasing.'[124] The controversy was only the public manifestation of his

[119] Jamieson, "Change of Position", 80.

[120] Bezzant, *Jonathan Edwards and the Church*, 28.

[121] Editor's Introduction, *WJE* 13:28.

[122] Editor's Introduction, *WJE* 14:39.

[123] Editor's Introduction, *WJE* 13:36.

[124] *WJE* 16:271.

personal long-term agonizing about the subject. As Minkema has pointed out, 'the "qualifications controversy" did not begin a mere four or five years before the actual fact; rather, its origins can be traced to the very outset of Edwards' ministry at Northampton.'[125]

Ultimately Edwards' concerns about the practice of the Lord's Supper in Northampton were rooted in his view of the nature of the Supper. The next two chapters will trace Edwards' theological understanding of the Supper and, in doing so, will reveal ideas about the Supper that did not sit easily with Stoddardeanism.

[125] Editor's Introduction, *WJE* 14:42.

Chapter Two
Remembering, Sealing, and Nourishing

As Danaher has observed 'historians generally agree that Edwards held the Lord's Supper in low esteem, in comparison to God-inspired, subjective affections, rejecting it as a unique "means" to the covenant of grace and the manifestation of the divine presence.'[1] This is because, as he continues, most of the focus has been upon the question of admission to the Supper given its prominence in the Communion Controversy that saw him removed from his pastorate. This impression is reinforced by the fact that Edwards' only treatises specifically about the Supper relate to the controversy. Yet, as Danaher points out, when we look at Edwards' sermon corpus we find a 'constructive theology' of the Lord's Supper.[2] Indeed, it is in the richness of his theology of the Lord's Supper, particularly expressed in his sermons, that his extremely high view of the sacrament can be seen and, it becomes clear, that his theology of the Supper must have made him uncomfortable with Northampton's admission policy long before the crisis broke in the 1740s.

Part of the reason that Edwards' sermons are such a rich source for considering his theology of the Lord's Supper is that its celebration was a regular feature of church life. It was celebrated every eight weeks and Edwards frequently took the opportunity to preach a sacrament sermon either in preparation for this, or at its celebration.[3] While the sermons were

[1]Danaher, "By Sensible Signs", 261.

[2]Danaher, "By Sensible Signs", 262.

[3]*WJE* 4:157. Edwards stated, 'our sacraments are eight weeks asunder.'

not treatises on the Supper, they were occasions to instruct and exhort the congregation to consider the significance of the meal in which they were to participate. In these addresses there was a profound sense of solemnity regarding the Supper, and warnings about eating unworthily, but it would be wrong to assume that his message was simply a negative one. Instead, Edwards sought to encourage his congregation to consider all that this meal represented and, in particular, the nature of the communion with Christ that it offered to them.

Edwards examined many themes that were prominent in the Protestant understanding of the Supper. In this chapter, we will begin to consider some of these as we examine his view of the Supper as an act of remembrance, a covenant seal, and a means of spiritual nourishment. The next chapter will consider how he viewed the Supper as a means of communion, both with Christ and between the saints.

The Lord's Supper as Remembrance

As Mayor has noted by the early seventeenth century among English Protestants 'The meaning of the Sacrament of the Lord's Supper was not in dispute at all.' As he goes on to point out, however, while this did not mean universal agreement on the matter quarreling 'over the Lord's Supper was a surprisingly minor issue.'[4] There appears to have been a widely held assumption that the meaning of the Lord's Supper was largely understood and agreed upon and, consequently, there was little attempt, as there had been in the early days of the Reformation, to offer a precise explanation of what occurred during its celebration. This is evident, for example, in Matthew Henry's popular 1704 work *The Communicant's Companion,* where little consideration is given to what transpired in the Supper. Rather, as Jong Hun Joo writes, 'Henry's concern on the Supper was not so much with the elements as with the state and life of the people attending the Supper.'[5] It was a trend that can be traced back to the sixteenth and seventeenth centuries where, as we have noted, English writers tended to place considerable emphasis on the spiritual condition of communicants.

As Mayor states there seemed to be a 'greater eagerness to exclude wrong understanding of the Eucharist than to inculcate right understanding.'[6] In

[4]Mayor, *The Lord's Supper*, 49.

[5]Joo, *Matthew Henry*, 138, 139.

[6]Mayor, *The Lord's* Supper, 84.

repudiating incorrect ideas about the Lord's Supper the chief target was usually the Mass and transubstantiation, even though this was no longer a threat to English Protestants. The Westminster Confession clearly rejected the Mass stating that 'The grace which is exhibited in or by the sacraments, rightly used, is not conferred by any power in them.'[7] Thomas Watson, commenting on the Confession, denied the Mass arguing 'it is absurd to imagine that the bread in the sacrament should be turned into Christ's flesh, and that his body which was hung before, should be made again of bread.'[8] The Savoy Declaration used the same wording as Westminster to renounce the Mass.

When it came to explaining the purpose of the Supper the emphasis was less on what was occurring in the sacrament, than upon the idea that it offered a representation of Christ's death that heightened the affections. As one of Edwards' Scottish correspondents, John Willison, put it Christ had instituted the Supper 'as a lively Resemblance and Memorial of his bloody Sufferings and Death in the Room of his people.'[9] The role of the Supper as a memorial was to draw the participant's mind back to Calvary in a way that stirred the heart. Thomas Watson stated that as Christ was remembered in the Supper 'We should not be able to look on Christ crucified with dry eyes.'[10] While Matthew Henry noted that in this meal 'Christ tells us earthly things, that thereby we may come to be more familiarly acquainted, and more warmly affected, with spiritual and heavenly things.'[11] The Supper was a memorial, but no one thought of it as a "bare" memorial. Rather, when Christ was remembered in the Supper it ought to be in a way that was deeply moving. As the Westminster Divine Richard Vines stated, 'If you exercise onely wit and invention, it's barren, but the exercise of affection is the best commemoration.'[12]

Edwards followed the tradition of viewing the Supper as a memorial. He wrote that it is 'a holy supper to be celebrated in remembrance of the Lord Christ and his redemption.'[13] His most sustained treatment of the theme of

[7] *Westminster Confession of Faith*, Chapter 27:3. Savoy Declaration of Faith, Chapter 28:3.

[8] Watson, *The Ten Commandments*, 226.

[9] Willison, *Sacramental Meditations*, 5.

[10] Watson, *The Ten Commandments,* 227.

[11] Henry, *Communicant's Companion,* 2.

[12] Vines, *Treatise of the Institution,* 161.

[13] *WJE* 17:239.

the sacrament as a memorial was in a sermon on the words of institution in Luke 22:19, 'This do in remembrance of me', preached before a celebration of the sacrament in 1734.[14] Edwards explained that with these words Jesus had established the Lord's Supper as an act of remembrance in anticipation of his impending death. While his immediate audience was the disciples, he was nonetheless giving instructions for 'all Christians to the End of the Time.' In his actions, in breaking the bread and drinking from the cup, he was exhorting them 'Do you as I have now done.' His purpose, in these words and actions, was to institute 'this Ordinance for his People to Remember him by when he is Gone.' Prior to this it was unnecessary because he was still with them. Edwards went on to point out that this meal was ordained at the Passover, and, at the same time, it marked the end of the Passover, since Christ by his death had abolished the Jewish dispensation and inaugurated the Christian era. He then stated the doctrine as 'The Lord's Supper is to be attended in Remembrance of Christ.'

As he developed the sermon, he first pointed out that the Supper was a duty to be fulfilled by Christians. Christ had commanded its observance and, therefore, it was incumbent upon Christians to obey his command in perpetuity. Here Edwards took the opportunity to point out that this was contrary to the view of the Quakers, a group he placed on a par with Catholics and Socinians,[15] who relegated the observance of the Supper to the early church. He drew attention to Paul's reminder in 1 Corinthians 11:26 that, in the Supper, Christians continue to remember Christ's death 'till he come.' Since Christ instituted this meal to remember him in his absence, then it was logical that its observance should last for the entire time of his absence. Furthermore, like all the commands of Christ, it was not constrained by any time limit. Nor was the command limited to any specific group, rather it was given to all Christians. In fact, he stated, 'No society of Christians Can Excuse themselves in omitting of it any more than they can excuse themselves from obeying Christ's other commands such as "love one another."'

The purpose of this memorial was to maintain the memory of Christ and his work, so that, throughout all time it would not be forgotten. Edwards said that many things had occurred in the past, even great events, which had no memorial, and they had been forgotten in subsequent generations. In the same way 'so might the whole story of Jesus Christ have been utterly

[14]No. 328. Luke 22:19, *WJEO* 49.

[15]*WJE* 9:431; *WJE* 17:369.

forgotten before this time had not God taken care to keep up the memory of it.' This Supper was appointed, along with Scripture, preaching and the Lord's Day, to maintain the memory of Christ and his work. Yet, for Edwards, while this historical record was important, it was not the only purpose that lay behind the memorial. It also had the goal of assisting Christians in meditating upon Christ and, especially, in keeping alive the memory of his death and reviving their hearts in this regard. As such its purpose was 'to fix our minds; to give us lively ideas of Christ and the things of Christ.' He made clear that this memorial was given to the church not just for the purpose of remembering him, 'but to Revive the thoughts of Christ in particular.' This memorial was a devotional aid for his people.

With this in mind, he explained that the Supper was not only directed at the understanding, but it also ought to stir 'suitable Exercises towards him in our Hearts.' We should, therefore 'Remember Christ in the Lord's supper Not with a Cold dull thought but with an affectionate Remembrance of him with Love to him, admiration of him, delight in him & desires after him.' In other words, for Edwards, the purpose of the Supper was to excite the participant's affections. As he noted in a 1745 sermon, which is perhaps his fullest and most mature expression of the nature of the Lord's Supper, it both instructs the mind and affects the heart.[16] Using language typical of the Puritans, he said that the Supper by 'lively representation' instructs, as well as the word of God. It does so by bringing Christ's death to the communicant's mind, fixing their contemplation upon him and so it affects the heart.

In the sermon on Luke 22:19 Edwards explained that this memorial meal was also a proclamation. He declared 'we should Testify our Respect to Christ in this Ordinance by Giving up our selves Entirely unto Jesus Christ making a solemn Renewed dedication of our selves to him.' This was another familiar theme among the Dissenters based on Paul's statement in 1 Corinthians 11:26, 'For as often as ye eat this bread, and drink this cup, ye do shew the Lord's death till he come.' As Matthew Henry put it, the Lord's Supper is a confessing ordinance in which 'we are said to show forth the Lord's death; that is, we hereby profess our value and esteem for Christ crucified.'[17] Similarly, for Edwards, the Supper was a testimony and declaration of the honor with which Christians hold Christ. This proclamation, however, was not only in the enacting of the sacrament but in the renewal of commitment to him.

[16]No. 791. 1 Corinthians 10:16(b), *WJEO* 63.

[17]Henry, *Communicant's Companion,* 23.

He then explained that Christ's principal design in the Supper was to draw attention to his 'last sufferings.' Edwards sought to bring this forcefully home to his congregation as he addressed them as the voice of Christ saying,

> [by] do this in remembrance of me he means do this in Remembrance [of] what I underwent for you. In Remembrance [of] what an Agony I was in in the Garden. How my soul was sorrowful even unto death. How I sweat when you do this Remembrance. How I was taken & handed, Arraigned & Condemned Like a malefactor when you do this Remembrance. Mocked spit upon & Buffeted by men. When how I was nailed on the Cross & there hung for hours together in Extreme Pain & torture. What dreadful sufferings I underwent in my soul when the Father was departed from me & when I Endured the terrible Effects of his wrath for your sakes. . . Remembering. . . how my blood was shed, my soul Poured out unto death.

It is not surprising, having portrayed such a vivid scene, he then declared that by remembering Christ's death in this way participants should be deeply 'affected with admiration for it was the most wonderful thing that Ever happened that so Great a Person for those that are so unworthy [was] affected with Love & Gratitude [and] affected with sorrow for our sins.'

Attempts to excite the congregation's affections in this way were typical of the Puritan tradition. Holifield writes that 'Puritan ministers uniformly described the Lord's Supper as a dramatic exhortation evoking appropriate mental states.'[18] For example, Richard Sibbes, a seventeenth century Anglican of Puritan persuasion, encouraged his congregation '[when] thou seest the Bread broken, and the Wine poured forth, this should stir thee up to be in the same estate, as if thou wert upon Golgotha, at the place whereupon he was crucified, crying with a loud voice, My God, my God, why hast thou forsaken me? As if thou sawest him sweat water and blood.'[19] While the Congregationalist John Owen exclaimed 'O that God in this ordinance would give our souls a view of him!'[20]

Having stated that remembering Christ's sufferings is the principal purpose of the Supper, Edwards added that it was also an occasion to remember the infinite excellence of his person while here on earth and his great love

[18]Holifield, *The Covenant Sealed,* 53.

[19]Sibbes, "The Right Receiving", 66.

[20]Quoted in Payne, *Owen Lord's Supper*, 65.

which was beyond parallel and was displayed in his going to the cross for 'Poor sinful miserable worms that were the object of that dying.' He then exhorted his hearers by asking, 'shall not we often Know it in our memories? Often think of it. Meditate upon it & Reviving an affecting sense of it Revive our Love & Gratitude to this our Father that hath so Loved us & hath so saved us?'

In his application, Edwards reminded his listeners that 'Christ is now absent from us as to his humble Person' and is no longer seen by human eyes as the disciples saw him. It was important, therefore, that his people 'Gladly make use of these visible Representations of him & signs of his dying love to us to Remember him.' Given the importance of the Supper as an act of remembrance he rebuked those 'that don't attend the sacrament [and] that disobey this Command.' This includes 'Persons that yet Call themselves Christians & would not be Ranked among the Heathen.' In other word, those who were nominal Christians. He used this language more explicitly in another sacramental sermon, where he spoke of those who are 'commonly called "the Christian [world]" in distinction to the heathens, Jews and Mahometans.'[21] He also rebuked those who did not come to the Supper to truly remember Christ but who only occasionally came to the sacrament because of some pang of conscience, when otherwise they lived careless lives and took no time to prepare themselves to eat and drink at the Lord's Table. With typical solemnity he warned them that when they did come to the Supper they did not 'do this in Remembrance of Christ but Rather do it to mock him & to trample on his body & blood & they do horribly abuse this sacred memorial of Christ's death & Eat & drink Judgement [Cf. I Cor. 11:29] to themselves.' It is clear from these rebukes that Edwards was aware of those who attended the Supper and were not properly qualified, either by profession or behavior as real Christians.

He concluded the sermon with three exhortations about the nature of remembrance. These were, first, to remember Christ so as to receive and embrace him in the ordinance. Second, to remember him in such a way as to engage to live for Christ and to follow his example. Finally, to remember him in order 'the more to unite our hearts to those that are his.'

This sermon gives us an insight into the multifaceted way in which Edwards thought about the Lord's Supper as a memorial meal. While it was a memorial it was not a "bare" memorial. Instead, it was designed to stimulate the affections and bring those who participated in it into a deeper

[21] *WJE* 14:462.

relationship with Christ. That it ought to increase the affections in this way is evident by the way that Edwards twice in his address put on the voice of Christ speaking directly to the congregation to look upon him in his suffering. The sermon also reveals something of the tension in his thought even at this early stage in his ministry in 1734. While the sacrament should revive the faith of Christ's people, it also rebuked those whose nominal Christianity meant that they were not suited to remembrance.

It is also clear that, for Edwards, the fact that the Supper was a memorial did not mean that Christ was absent. This had been one of the issues that critics had latched onto surrounding the memorialism proposed by Zwingli, where he was accused of simply considering Christ's death as a historic event and, consequently, considering Christ to be entirely absent from the sacrament. While it might be debated whether this is a true representation of Zwingli's views, it was not the type of memorialism that Edwards espoused. This is seen in the Luke 22:19 sermon and from another sermon preached in 1743 on Matthew 9:15, 'Can the Children of the bride chamber mourn as long as the bridegroom is with them?'[22] Here he pointed out that when Christ died and was laid in the grave, his disciples were sorrowful. The disciples, however, saw this bodily absence differently in the aftermath of the Resurrection and the Ascension. Then they came to understand that when 'Christ ascended he was taken from 'em again as to his bodily presence yet it was but in order to [experience] a more abundant spiritual presence which was more comfortable & Joyfull than meerly his bodily Presence.' Edwards went on to state the doctrine of his sermon as 'when a Company or society of Christians have Christ present with them 'tis the greatest cause of Joy to them.'

He then set out the ways in which Christ might be said to be with his people. There was a sense in which Christ was always present with a person once they were converted and they became a temple of the Holy Spirit. There were other occasions when Christ may be said to be with his people by means of special tokens of his presence. Then, there was also a sense in which Christ might be said to withdraw his presence when his people drove him away because of their behavior. In the light of this, Edwards urged his congregants to ensure that Christ was present with them, not least in the celebration of the Lord's Supper, where his presence would produce joy because 'If Christ be Present with us it will be the greatest cause of joy, it will make that feast joyful to us above all things in the world.' If, however,

[22]No. 668. Matthew 9:15(b), *WJEO* 59.

'we come to the Lord's supper & find nothing of Christ there & don't meet with him we shall [have] reason to go away mourning & with heavy hearts.' If Christ was present at the Supper, then they 'may go from the table with a sweet & Joyful remembrance of the appearance.'

For Edwards remembrance did not exclude communion with Christ. Rather, Christ was present at the memorial feast, and the act of remembrance stirred the heart. As he told his congregation in his Luke 22:19 sermon merely having 'a thought of Christ in our minds without any good effect of it in our hearts is to no purpose.' As he continued 'we ought to remember Christ in the Lord's Supper not with a cold dull thought but with an affectionate remembrance of him with love to him [and] admiration of him.'[23] This sense that Christ was present at the Supper was an occasion to try to rouse the affections of his congregation.

This rousing of the affections involved not only Edwards' stirring rhetoric concerning the knowledge of Christ's presence but also the drama of the Supper itself. While the Reformers had tended to play down the spectacle of the Supper, given the way in which it had taken center stage in the medieval Church, they nonetheless recognized that properly understood its celebration was a drama. As Benjamin Griffith points out the Reformers retained the idea of the Supper as a drama, but they shifted its focus through their 'historicizing tendency' as they placed their emphasis 'on re-imagining rather than re-experiencing the sacrifice.'[24] For example, Calvin noted that God did permit images but only 'those living symbols which the Lord has consecrated by his word: I mean Baptism and the Lord's Supper, with other ceremonies. By these our eyes ought to be more steadily fixed, and more vividly impressed, than to require the aid of any images which the wit of man may devise.'[25] The sacraments 'represent promises to the life, as if painted in a picture.'[26]

In England the Supper was also viewed as a drama. As Julia Houston notes Cranmer 'turned the 'miracle' of the Lord's Supper into a drama.'[27] While Jon Payne has described John Owen's view of the Supper as 'a sanctified dramatization of the love of God for His people'[28] As Hunt remarks, 'The

[23]No. 328. Luke 22:19, *WJEO* 49.

[24]Griffith, *Playing the Past*, 27.

[25]Calvin, *Institutes,* I. xi.13.

[26]Calvin, *Institutes,* IV. xiv.5.

[27]Houston, "Transubstantiation and the Sign", 113.

[28]Payne, *Owen Lord's Supper*, 15.

fact that the sacrament could be touched, tasted and seen gave it a power of physical suggestiveness which even the preaching of the word lacked.'[29] The result was, as Susan Hardman Moore writes, 'Dissenting worship was not a sensory desert (as is often assumed), but used the senses—and imagery that drew on the senses—to cultivate an intensity that imbued everything with sacred meaning.'[30]

Some Reformed writers saw the role played by the minister in the Supper as representing God's actions in salvation. For example, William Perkins viewed the actions of the minister in the administration of the Supper as reflecting God's own actions stating, 'The action of the minister is a note of God's action.' Each of the minister's actions 'seal the action of God the Father.[31] Similarly, Robert Bolton, a conforming Puritan, saw in the minister's actions a representation of "the spirituall, eternall, and invisible actions of God the Father, for the God of our Soule.'[32] Calvin viewed the minister as standing in Christ's place. Wolterstorff writes,

> Calvin seems to understand the relations between the signifying actions of presider and people and the signified actions. By declaring "this is Christ's body given for you" over the bread, and "this is Christ's blood shed for you" over the wine, the presider ascribes signifying import to the bread and wine and to his action of offering them. When the presider then does actually offer the bread and the wine to the communicants, that counts as the flesh-and-blood Jesus Christ offering himself. By the presider doing that, Jesus Christ does that.[33]

English Dissenters came to think of the Supper as a rehearsal of the Last Supper. Martha Finch writes that 'Descriptions of the Lord's Supper in separatist churches in England and Amsterdam illustrate how the sacramental actions plainly—immediately and accurately—reenacted what participants understood to be Christ's and his disciples' behavior at the Last Supper.'[34] We see an example of this approach in the words of John Willison who gave

[29]Hunt, "The Lord's Supper", 59.

[30]Moore, "Worship and Sacraments", 427.

[31]Perkins, *A Golden Chain,* 167.

[32]Quoted in Webster, *Godly Clergy,* 114.

[33]Wolterstorff, "John Calvin", 109.

[34]Finch, *Dissenting Bodies,* 159.

detailed instructions about the role of the minister in communion, where he saw his actions as being modeled on those of Christ at the Last Supper. He stated that his actions were four-fold 'as may be seen in Christ's Example, 1. He took Bread. 2. He blessed the Bread and Wine. 3. He brake the Bread. 4. He gave both of them to his Disciples.'[35] He went on to explain that each of these actions was based upon Christ's actions on that evening. For example, the bread should be broken as instituted by Christ, and the bread and wine passed from hand to hand as had happened on the first celebration. He instructed his congregation that when they saw the minister handle the elements during the Supper they should 'Take a view of Jesus on the cross, breathing forth love to us, when he was breathing forth his last; let us look straightly and steadfastly to him as he did to us... when you see the bread broken, look to Christ's open wounds as an open city of refuge for thy soul.'[36] As Holifield observes 'Puritan ministers had insisted that the celebration of the sacraments be visible to congregations, believing that the elements and gestures were providentially adapted to move the mind through the senses.'[37]

Edwards continued in this tradition of seeing in the celebration of the Supper an element of dramatic re-enactment, which he again viewed as an opportunity to heighten the affections of the participants. This drama included not only a focus upon the sufferings as Edwards impersonated Christ in his pleadings, but also in his view of Christ as the actual minister of the sacrament, with the presiding minister in his place offering the sacrament to the congregation, just as Christ had given it to the disciples at its first celebration. This was something he alluded to in the Luke 22:19 sermon when he stated that when thinking of the Supper 'we must Look upon Christ as speaking to them as minister' of the sacrament and the disciples as those appointed as ministers.[38]

It is an idea to which he returned on other occasions. In a sacrament sermon on Ezekiel 23.37–39, Edwards dealt with the nature of ordinances in general and 'the Ordinances of God's house or Publick worship.'[39] Such ordinances were administered in God's name by authorized ministers. When the minister preached, he was heard as 'one representing Christ' and 'in

[35]Willison, *A Sacramental Catechism,* 69.

[36]Willison, *A Sacramental Directory, 234.*

[37]Holifield, *The Covenant* Sealed, 138.

[38]No. 328. Luke 22:19, *WJEO* 49.

[39]No. 222. Ezekiel 23:37–39, *WJEO* 49.

administering sacraments the minister represents the person of Christ [and] in the Lord's supper stands in Christ's stead.' In another sermon on 1 Corinthians 10:17, as he explored the nature of the Supper as a seal, Edwards explained that it was a seal on Christ's part. As such 'The minister acts in that ordinance as Christ's representative.' Notably, he did so when he imitated Christ's actions at the inauguration of the Supper. He continued,

> The minister's actions in breaking [bread], pouring out [wine], and offering [them] are appointed as an open declaration and confirmation of the act of his heart, that he fully and freely consents to, and complies with, his part of the covenant. The union of his heart to his people exhibits his dying love, his readiness to receive them into that near relation, into a vital union.[40]

While his approach of seeing the Supper as a historic dramatization had its precedents, he seemed to take this further by his particular emphasis upon Christ as the minister of the sacrament through the actions of the presiding minister. While previous generations of Protestants may have been fearful of the minister being perceived as acting in a priestly manner it was, for Edwards, simply a logical extension of the role of the minister tying the audible and visible words of God together. If 'when the word is preached by authorized ministers they speak in God's name'[41] then, in the same way, since the Supper is 'a kind of visible word'[42] the minister was again acting in Christ's place. Such a concept of Christ as the minister of the sacrament was a further means of dramatizing the Supper and stirring the participants' affections by remembering that he was present as they took the bread and wine.

In a 1733 sermon on 1 Corinthians 11:29, 'For he that eateth and drinketh unworthily, eateth and drinketh damnation to himself, not discerning the Lord's body' Edwards developed the idea of the minister as Christ's representative. He stated that while 'all God's ordinances are in some Respects alike holy... the sacrament of the Lord's supper seems to be more Eminently sacred & holy.' The reason for this eminence in sanctity was Christ 'more Especially as being then & there Present.'[43] He noted that this was because

[40]*WJE* 25:587.

[41]No. 222. Ezekiel 23:37–39, *WJEO* 46.

[42]No. 791. 1 Corinthians 10:16(b), *WJEO* 63.

[43]No. 270. 1 Corinthians 11:29, *WJEO* 48.

Christ was present in the person of the minister, who was to be 'Looked upon as though Christ stood there offering it to us & therein offering us his Benefits.' Christ was also considered to be especially present as his body and blood were represented and, as such, he was 'Present to our bodily Eyes & not only to our Eyes but to our Other senses, to our touch & taste, besides our seeing with our Eyes the outward signs & tokens of his body & blood we do in this ordinance as it were handle Christ.' Edwards saw beyond Christ's spiritual presence and pointed to him being present to the physical senses of the communicant. He went on to add that it was in his death that Christ was especially present in the sacrament as 'not only sensibly Represented as being Present amongst us but as being slain amongst us.' Again, we see how he viewed the Supper as particularly drawing attention to Christ in his last sufferings.

Speaking in this way Edwards went beyond the sacramental tradition that he had inherited. While many in this tradition stated that Christ was especially present at the Supper, there was little explanation of the sense in which this was the case. The Puritan minister Stephen Charnock wrote 'We have not so near a communion with a person, either by petitioning for something we want, or returning him thanks for a favor received, as we have by sitting with him at his table, partaking of the same bread and the same cup.'[44] Yet, he offered no explanation of why the Supper offered particularly close communion. Likewise, John Owen in his discourses on the sacrament spoke of how in the Supper there was 'an especial and peculiar communion with Christ' and 'the special communion which the believers have with Christ in the ordinance'[45] but again without explanation. Edwards, however, emphasized that Christ was present in the person of the minister not as a priest, but as a representative and historic re-enactor.

He also viewed Christ as present because of the physical presence of the bread and wine. Edwards' emphasis on the engagement of all the senses in the Supper may reflect the growing move towards, what Holifield has termed, the 'piety of sensation.'[46] Here, Belden Lane detects the influence of John Smith and other Cambridge Platonists where 'One receives a new capacity to embrace a "sensible idea"—to experience spiritual realities with all the vividness of a sense impression, whether visual, auditory, palatal,

[44]Charnock, "A Discourse", 407.

[45]Payne, *Owen Lord's Supper*, 95, 104.

[46]Holifield, *The Covenant* Sealed, 135.

tactile, or olfactory.'[47] A similar emphasis is found in the work of Matthew Henry who wrote,

> We live in a *World of Sense*, not yet in the *World of Spirits*; and because we therefore find it hard to look above the *things that are seen*, we are directed in a sacrament to look *through* them to those things *not seen* that are represented by them. That things meerly sensible may not improve the Advantage they have from our present State wholly to engross our Thoughts and in compassion to our infirmity Spiritual Things are in this ordinance made in a manner sensible.[48]

Yet, there was an older Reformed tradition that lay behind this. As Holifield points out William Perkins considered the sacraments as 'worship of the body' while the Puritans insisted that they 'impressed themselves upon the five senses.'[49] Andrew Gray, a seventeenth century Scottish minister, assured his congregation that when they ate by faith it satisfied their senses of sight taste and touch.[50] Edwards took such ideas further and, as Lane writes, 'He perceived the physical world, when appreciated with the new spiritual sense that regeneration brings, as offering direct training in the multidimensional way of knowing that is necessary for meeting God. This is a knowing that involves a tasting and delighting—not just an apprehension of the mind, but an intimate engagement of all the senses as well.'[51]

Edwards continued in the Protestant and Puritan tradition of viewing the Lord's Supper as a memorial meal. Yet, it is evident, he did not think in terms of a "bare" memorialism. The act of remembrance was there as an aid to stir the affections as the Supper was celebrated in a dramatic form, as if it were Christ himself who was present, presiding and displaying the food and drink. The Supper was a celebration not only of Christ's death but of his presence. This sense of Christ's presence, while not less than spiritual communion, went beyond the spiritual to his being physically present to all the senses of the communicant.

[47]Lane, *Ravished by Beauty*, 183.

[48]Henry, *Communicant's Companion*, 2.

[49]Holifield, *The Covenant Sealed*, 49.

[50]Gray, *Mystery of Faith*, 93. Todd, *Culture of Protestantism*, 101.

[51]Lane, *Ravished by Beauty*, 179.

The Lord's Supper as Covenant Seal

Part of the way in which the Reformed tradition thought of the Supper as a memorial was that it functioned as a seal. Many Reformed authors spoke of the sacraments as seals, yet, as Holifield remarks, 'It was not always clear, however, what was meant by calling a sacrament a covenant seal [and it]... proved susceptible to various interpretations.'[52] Calvin thought in terms of the sacraments as seals of God's promise, writing 'never is a sacrament without an antecedent promise, the sacrament being added as a kind of appendix, with the view of confirming and sealing the promise, and giving a better attestation, or rather, in a manner, confirming it.'[53] In Calvin's mind, the seal was like the official seals that were found 'affixed to diplomas, and other public deeds.'[54] While the Puritans continued to use the language of sealing, as Holifield points out, this involved 'a departure in tone and emphasis from Calvin.' In particular they 'tended to rely on subjective elements of sacramental efficacy.'[55] William Ames, for example, wrote 'The primary end of a Sacrament is to seal the Covenant; and that is not on God's part only, but consequently it is also on ours; that is, not only are the grace of God and his promises sealed to us, but also our thankfulness and obedience are sealed towards God.'[56] Among New England Puritans the sacraments were primarily thought of in terms of covenant seals. On several occasions in his work, *The Way of Congregational Churches Cleared* John Cotton simply referred to the sacraments as 'the seals.'[57]

Given this heritage, it is not surprising to find that the idea of sealing played a prominent part in Edwards' understanding of the Supper. As Danaher comments, 'he maintained throughout his life a belief that the Lord's Supper was a "seal of the Covenant."'[58] He viewed the Supper as a seal both in the sense that Calvin used the concept and in the later Puritan sense. Like Calvin, he saw it as a seal of God's promise writing that 'Christ by his death confirmed His doctrine. His Testimony & His Promises. So

[52]Holifield, *The Covenant Sealed,* 26.

[53]Calvin, *Institutes,* IV. xiv.3.

[54]Calvin, *Institutes,* IV. xiv. 5.

[55]Holifield, *The Covenant Sealed,* 53.

[56]Ames, *The Marrow of Theology*, 198, 199.

[57]Ziff, *John Cotton*, e.g., 262, 324.

[58]Danaher, "By Sensible Signs", 262.

all These are Sealed in this representation of his death.[59] Going on to explain the nature of a seal he said 'a seal is an appointed sign by which any Person confirms & establishes some act of his concerning some other Person.' Like the Puritans, he noted that there was mutual sealing in the sacrament, 'Wherein we are mutually concurring both are active in covenanting. There are promises on both sides. Both therefore Do seal & Confirm the Covenant.' With this in mind, when he spoke of the Lord's Supper as a seal, there was a strong emphasis on the mutual obligations of the covenant. The Supper was not only a sign of God's participation in the covenant but also those who shared in the Supper sealed their own participation in it. Preaching on Jeremiah 42:20 he said, 'Persons that Come to the Lord's Supper and take his body and blood do in the most solemn manner possible vow that they will be the Lord's and that they set their hand and seal to the Covenant thereby and they take the body and blood of Christ in token that they will take Christ for their Lord and Saviour and that they will obey his Commandments.'[60]

This mutual sealing also reflected friendship, so that the sacrament was a 'spiritual feast which God has provided in Jesus Christ for our souls with such great expense, and to signify and seal the covenant with agreement and friendship between God and his people.'[61] In this way, the Supper was an act of covenant renewal where, as God renewed his covenant with his people, they renewed their covenantal vows to him. In the sacramental sermon on 1 Corinthians 11:29, Edwards stated there is 'herein a mutual covenanting between God and us [which] is most solemnly renewed and sealed. This mutual covenanting that there is between God and his people is never more solemnly transacted than it is in this ordinance.'[62] In the Supper, Christ renewed the offer of himself, and the benefits obtained by his death, while believers solemnly professed their acceptance of him.

The fact that the Supper was an act of covenant renewal for the participants also offered opportunities for Edwards to rebuke his congregation and urge them to strain for a life of greater godliness. In a sacrament sermon preached in 1741 on Psalm 72:6, 'He shall come down like rain upon the mown grass' Edwards told his hearers of their need to be cut down with a sense of Evangelical humiliation. He also urged them to relinquish 'carnal ease and other carnal things.' They must do 'as you have vowed you will do

[59]No. 791. 1 Corinthians 10:16(b), *WJEO* 63.

[60]No. 094. Jeremiah 42:20, *WJEO* 43.

[61]*WJE* 14:288.

[62]No. 270. 1 Corinthians 11:29, *WJEO* 48.

in that solemn covenant you have entered into with God, which covenant you have sealed this day in your partaking at the Lord's table.'[63]

Edwards' most extensive treatment of the nature of the Supper as a seal came in a sermon preached at Stockbridge during a visit in 1751. The extent to which he dealt with the nature of sealing is perhaps surprising because, as Wilson H. Kimnach notes, it was composed 'on the spot, apparently because he had not brought such a sermon with him and the congregation wished to celebrate the sacrament.'[64] The text that Edwards chose on this occasion for his English and Indian congregation was 1 Corinthians 10:17, 'For we being many are one body, and one bread: for we are all partakers of that one bread.' After a very brief comment on the text, which may indicate the *ad hoc* character of the sermon, he outlined four points on the nature of union with Christ before stating the doctrine '*The Lord's Supper was instituted as a solemn representation and seal of the holy and spiritual union of Christ's people [to] Christ, and one to another*.'[65] Edwards then developed the sermon by pointing to the union between Christ and his people, offering as his first proposition 'Christ's people are strictly united to Christ and one to another.' This union had a relative, legal, and vital dimension but 'an union of hearts is the foundation of all.'[66] As a consequence of this union between Christ and his people, Christians were united to each other, with him as their head. This led Edwards to conclude, 'Consequent on those things, there must be a sweet harmony among all the members as to temper and as to conversation; and a natural inclination to sweet society and mutual converse one with another.'[67]

Edwards' second proposition developed this idea further as he noted that 'The Lord's Supper is a solemn representation and seal' that displays the union between Christ and his people and between the people themselves. He proceeded to explain that a seal was 'some sign or token exhibited by any person or persons as a solemn, explicit confirmation of the thing sealed as what they profess to be their own act.' His language echoed the sense in which Calvin spoke of the Supper as an official seal, although he did not develop the concept in the same way. Instead, he continued it 'seals of the covenant between Christ and his people. His seal confirms [the covenant]

[63] *WJE* 22:316.

[64] Editor's Introduction, *WJE* 25:582.

[65] *WJE* 25: 585.

[66] *WJE* 25: 585.

[67] *WJE* 25: 586.

as his own free act, [or] the free compliance of his heart; and his peoples as their act, [a] testimony of the free compliance of their hearts.'[68]

He then explored the mutual nature of the seal by arguing that it acted both as a seal on Christ's part and on the part of his people. Once more, he explained that since there were two parties engaged in the act of sealing the minister acted on Christ's part, and through his actions at the table, he made an 'open declaration and confirmation of the act of [Christ's] heart, that he fully and freely consents to, and complies with, his part of the covenant. The union of his heart to his people exhibits his dying love, his readiness to receive them into that near relation, into a vital union.' For Christ's people, when they took the bread and wine, they made 'a solemn declaration and open testimony and confirmation that they do make this part of the covenant, that they comply with the condition required of them; that as Christ offers, they accept.' Edwards viewed this as 'the most solemn confirmation that can be conceived of.'[69] Since it was a mutual sealing he remarked "tis just in this ordinance as 'tis in the mutual tokens of consent and acceptance in marriage.'[70] For Edwards the Supper served as a means of covenant renewal for both parties.

When it came to the sermon's application Edwards worked out the implications of this concept of sealing. In this post-Northampton context, he was able to declare these in explicit terms. He began by stating boldly that 'such as know that they have no such union with Christ and his people ought not to come to this ordinance. How great and palpable is the absurdity [of such a practice].' He continued in an equally strident tone asking, 'Will any be so absurd as to say that God has appointed a holy ordinance of his worship for his honor and glory on purpose that men might openly and most expressly, and on deliberation and design and with the greatest solemnity, perjure themselves after this manner?' Logically, there could be no participation in this meal that solemnized the union between Christ and his people where no such union existed. As he made clear, in a statement reflecting on the practice of his grandfather and the church in Northampton, 'the design is not to make men children [who] ben't admitted into the family that they may be received into the family.' Likewise, in terms of the meal as a celebration of the union between believers and a seal of their Christian friendship, he asked 'how can they come and seal such friendship who are

[68]*WJE* 25: 587.

[69]*WJE* 25:587.

[70]*WJE* 25:588.

no friends, seal peace who have never made their peace?'[71] In a similar vein, he asked 'I would observe that sacraments are covenant privileges and benefits, and was there ever any such thing known in any nation as a man's having a right to the benefits of any covenant or benefit but only by virtue of fulfilling the conditions of it?'[72] While the sermon might have been to a Stockbridge community containing many Indians, who it is doubtful would have grasped the allusions in Edwards' arguments to his recent dispute in Northampton, he continued to defend his stance on the Lord's Supper. The fact that the sermon was composed on the spot may also have laid bare the rawness of the preacher's feelings in light of the recent controversy.

What is evident once more from this sermon is that Edwards thought in terms of Christ's presence at the sacrament. With the minister acting as his representative, there was a real covenant renewal on Christ's part. The congregation, in this way, also renewed their covenant with Christ. The covenant meal was not merely a memorial to a historic covenant established by Christ, but it was a vital transaction between him and his people each time it was celebrated. This reflected Edwards' view of the true church as 'united with Christ as his bride, his mystical body, in some way that involves a metaphysically real union between the two.'[73]

The sermon also begs the question of how long Edwards had thought of the sealing of the covenant in this way, believing that those who participated in the Supper but had never made their peace with God, ought not to come to the ordinance. Certainly, the language of mutual sealing is evident in some early sermons such the one on Jeremiah 42:20. Also as the sermon on 1 Corinthians 11:29 stated those who eat and drink 'receive and embrace Jesus Christ, they eat and drink their salvation because they receive the Savior' in an act of covenant sealing.[74] It seems that there was throughout his ministry an inescapable tension in Edwards' view of what sealing involved and who could engage in that act and the possibility that the Supper could also act as a converting ordinance.

[71] *WJE* 25:588.

[72] *WJE* 25:589.

[73] Crisp, "Closing of the Table", 58.

[74] *WJE* 17:271.

The Lord's Supper as Spiritual Nourishment

The Supper not only served as a memorial and an act of covenant renewal, but it was also a means of spiritual nourishment because Christ was present. The view of the Supper as a means of spiritual nourishment was deeply embedded in Reformed thinking. Calvin saw the Supper in this way stating in the *Institutes* 'Christ is therein given us for food, we perceive that without him we fail, pine, and waste away, just as hunger destroys the vigor of the body.' Consequently, all 'like persons famishing, should come to the feast.'[75] The design of the feast was 'to nourish our spiritual life.'[76] The importance of the feast as a means of spiritual nurture led Calvin to advocate weekly communion.[77] The idea of the Supper as a means of spiritual nurture continued to play a prominent part in the Reformed churches. William Perkins described the Supper as being for 'the full and perfect nourishment of our souls',[78] while William Ames referred to it as 'the Sacrament of the nourishing and growth of the faithful in Christ.'[79] When, one of Edwards' favorite authors, the Dutch theologian Petrus van Mastricht came to deal with the sacraments in his work *Theoretica Practica Theologia,* having titled the section on baptism *De Sacramentis Regenerationis,* the sacrament of regeneration, he called his treatment of the Lord's Supper *De Sacramentis Nutritionis*, the sacrament of nutrition.[80] Another favorite European author, Francis Turretin, explained 'the holy Supper seals our spiritual nourishment and support by Christ, in memory of his death, in which he prepared for us the food of life by which we are sustained.'[81]

The idea of the sacrament as a means of spiritual nutrition was also prominent in New England. John Cotton said the Supper 'yeelds plentifull nourishment.' In more vivid language he wrote how in the sacrament 'there is bread to strengthen weak grace, and wine to quicken dull spirits.' All of

[75] Calvin, *Institutes,* IV. xvii.42.

[76] Calvin, *Institutes,* IV. xvii.3.

[77] Calvin, *Institutes,* IV. xvii.44, 46. The Genevan authorities rejected this idea. Others in the English Reformed tradition, such as John Owen and Thomas Goodwin, also advocated a weekly celebration. Edwards too was in favor of its weekly celebration, *WJE* 16:366.

[78] Perkins, *A Reformed Catholic,* 86.

[79] Ames, *The Marrow of Theology*, 212.

[80] Mastricht, *Theoretico-practica Theologia,* 815, 828.

[81] Turretin, *Elenctic Theology,* 574.

which made the Christian 'come to the sacrament thirsting after Christ.'[82] The influential New England minister Thomas Shepard said that the Supper signified 'The body and blood of Christ crucified, offered and given to nourish and strengthen believers, renewing their faith unto eternal life.' He added that it followed from this 'it is the sacrament of our growth in Christ, being new born, because it is food given to nourish us, having received life... therefore it is to be administered and received often, that we may grow.'[83] Like their British and European counterparts, the New England ministers tended to be better at stating that the Supper spiritually nourished believers than explaining how it was able to do this and how it did so in a distinctive way.

The idea of the Supper as spiritual nourishment played a significant role in Edwards' understanding of the sacrament. In a 1734 sermon on Luke 14:16, 'Then said he unto him, A certain man made a great supper and bade many', he explained how 'The spiritual blessings of the gospel are fitly represented by a feast.' He described how participants 'as it were eat [Christ's] flesh and drink his blood.' Christ, as he went on to note, is 'the entertainment.'[84] He used the term entertainment, in its now archaic sense, to mean food and drink. This naturally raised the question of how a person feasted upon Christ and was nurtured by him. Edwards explained that this entertainment was 'Jesus Christ, with his benefits that he purchased by his obedience and death, and which he communicates by his Spirit.' These benefits included 'such as sanctification, spiritual knowledge, the manifestation of God's favor, peace of conscience, joy in the Holy Ghost and the exercises of holiness in good works.'[85] A person was nurtured through their participation in the Supper, not by directly feeding upon Christ, but with the aid of the Holy Spirit as they remembered again what Christ had accomplished for them through his death.

For Edwards, there was a particular aptness in God's provision of a meal as the means of remembrance. This was because the gospel 'nourishes the soul as food does the body... it gives life and strength to it.'[86] Also, the actual elements of bread and wine were eminently suitable for the meal. He wrote, 'God's wisdom is to be seen in the choice of the elements: the

[82]Cotton, *The Way of Life*, 365, 366.

[83]Shepard, "Christian Religion", 350.

[84]*WJE* 14:282.

[85]*WJE* 14:282.

[86]*WJE* 14:284.

bread, which is the staff of life, which best signifies that spiritual life and nourishment which we have in Christ, and which best signifies the body of Christ, that bread which came down from heaven; and the wine, which best signifies the spiritual joy and delight which the church hath in Jesus Christ.'[87]

Furthermore, this meal was fitting because it was more than a meal, it was a feast. Ninety-six times in the sermon Edwards referred to the Supper as a feast. Here he saw beyond the simplicity of the bread and wine to consider the cost at which the entertainment provided by God was obtained which was 'at no less a rate than with the blood of his only and infinitely dear Son.'[88] He also remarked 'We call those meals "feasts", where the provision is what excels ordinary food. The provision that God has made for our souls in Christ is exceeding excellent.'[89] He referred to that which God had provided in Christ as 'dainties', an older English term for culinary delicacies. Also, the meal was suitably called a feast because 'of the abundance and variety of it. There is every kind of blessing for our souls provided in the gospel that we need, so that we may want nothing at all, but may have every regular appetite and desire satisfied and we may be made completely [happy].'[90] For Edwards, the meal as a feast was a suitable depiction of the gospel because it represented how 'sinners are freely invited to partake of gospel blessings.'[91] Here the poor sinner, in the words of the prophet Isaiah, came 'without money and without price' and participated in 'a royal feast, the feast of a king.'[92]

His sermon exudes a sense, not only of the richness and abundance of the benefits of the gospel, but also how these things are appropriately represented in the feast of the Lord's Supper. There can be little doubt that he was using the sermon to rouse his congregation from what he considered to be their spiritual lethargy. Indeed, at one point he exclaimed 'O, what reason have we [to] admire the wonderful grace of God herein!' He then went on to invite them to participate in the feast while also addressing them with several questions,

[87] *WJE* 14:289.

[88] *WJE* 14:282.

[89] *WJE* 14:284.

[90] *WJE* 14:285.

[91] *WJE* 14:283.

[92] *WJE* 14:285.

> Don't it move you at all, therefore, what provision God has made for you, what glorious entertainment he has provided for you? Have you no heart to accept of the invitation? Is it not worth the while to be taken from hedges and dunghills and to be clothed with wrought gold and jewels, to dwell in a palace and sit at a prince's table? Is it not worth the while to accept of any invitation to come to the marriage supper of the Lamb?[93]

It is not clear who exactly Edwards had in mind as he asked these pointed questions. Was it neglectful believers? Or those who took the Supper without an explicit profession of faith? If the latter, then it may have been the case that while not committed to the idea of the Supper as a converting ordinance, he at least acknowledged that it might nonetheless incidentally fulfill that role.

What is evident is that, for Edwards, the Supper was a wonderful illustration of the benefits obtained by Christ which were now available to the believer. Here they could receive real spiritual nourishment for their soul. This nourishment came through the remembrance of Christ's death and the reappropriation by faith of the benefits of the gospel as represented by the bread and the wine. The richness and abundance of the feast spoke to the participants of the plentiful supply of blessings that God had provided through Christ.

Edwards also developed the theme of how a person is nourished by the Supper in another sacrament sermon preached on Psalm 78:25, 'Man did Eat Angels food.' Here he noted how the food provided for the Israelites in the wilderness was described in the Psalm as 'the corn of heaven', 'angel's food', and elsewhere as the 'bread of heaven.' He pointed out that this could not be literal food since angels are spiritual beings who do not need physical nourishment. Consequently, the Psalm was an example of typology, where the 'manna represented Christ with his benefits which is the true bread from heaven and is indeed angels' food.' He then considered how Christians were nourished through the sacrament by spiritually feeding upon Christ. He stated that this was done in two senses 'Either in having the possession and enjoyment of the Person of Christ and partaking of the benefits which he [purchased] or feed[ing] on Christ in [the] blessedness in the person of Christ.'[94] It was this second sense in which a person was nourished by Christ that he went on to develop.

[93]*WJE* 14:290.

[94]No. 206. Psalm 78:25, *WJEO* 46.

He explained that someone fed upon the person of Christ as they spiritually beheld his glory and divine excellency. Once more, he compared this spiritual feeding to physical nourishment, noting that the believer lived spiritually by 'viewing of the Beauty of Jesus Christ as the body lives by food. So, when the believer sees the divine beauty of Christ it refreshes his inward man; it rejoices his heart; it quiets his soul.' The result of feeding upon Christ in this way was that it 'begets and draws forth gracious inclinations and desires and holy affection and enables [him] to perform truly gracious and holy actions and to bring forth fruit unto holiness. To walk and run in the ways of God's commandments and be of a heavenly conversation.' He saw this process operating as the believer contemplated the excellency of Christ and, by this means, stimulated the holy principle that is operational in the heart of Christians. In this sense, they were like the angels in heaven who live upon God in contemplation of his glory and excellency. He noted that they did so 'by their seeing & understanding of it.' He did not have in mind a mystical contemplation of God, rather for people, like angels, 'knowledge is the food of the understanding especially the knowledge of great and worthy objects.' He added that Christ's excellency was especially seen in his word and his works, notably the work of redemption.

Under this heading, he also explained that an individual fed upon Christ's person by being 'happy in his love.' Happiness was a major theme for Edwards who saw it as 'the highest end of the creation of the universe' where God had 'created the world for this very end, to make the creature happy in his love.'[95] This happiness came through Christ's love and was the result of being in union and communion with him. Such communion refreshed, enlivened, and strengthened the soul. This communion was demonstrated by the very human act of eating which indicated both partaking of Christ in faith and loving him.

Edwards then turned his attention to how a person was nourished by the Supper through partaking of the benefits which Christ purchased by his death. He pointed out that this was what Scripture particularly meant by 'partaking of Christ's body and blood.' Here he took time to comment that this was not literally eating and drinking the body and blood, but it was as if the benefits procured by Christ in his death were received by eating and drinking his body and blood. In this sense, believers were again like angels who were joyfully fed and entertained by contemplating Christ's work in redemption. He noted that 'The benefits of Christ's purchase which believers

[95] *WJE* 13:200, 336.

partake of are of the same kind with the blessings that the angels enjoy in heaven. 'Tis the favor of the same God. The same kind of eternal life. The same riches. The same kind of honors and pleasures that the angels do enjoy.' Although, he also pointed out, the angels do not participate in the benefits of Christ's work in the same way as human beings.

Edwards' explanation of how Christians are nourished by the Supper touches upon key themes in his wider writings. As Douglas Sweeney writes 'For Edwards, Christ stood at the center of God's purpose in the creation and redemption of the world— a kind of cosmic keystone, or better, an infinite source of love binding the universe together.'[96] As such there was no higher goal for any creature, in heaven or on earth, than to contemplate the excellency of Christ. This was something that the Supper allowed a person to do as they meditated upon Christ while they ate and drank. It was, however, only a regenerated person who was able to see the excellency of Christ since only they had received the Holy Spirit as 'an indwelling vital principle.'[97] With this new principle came a new sense of the heart by which a person experienced 'a true sense of the divine excellency of the things revealed in the Word of God, and a conviction of the truth and reality of them, thence arising.' For Edwards, the Supper appeared as an ideal means for a person to experience what he described as 'a real sense and apprehension of the divine excellency of things revealed in the Word of God. A spiritual and saving conviction of the truth and reality of these things, [which] arises from such a sight of their divine excellency and glory; so that this conviction of their truth is an effect and natural consequence of this sight of their divine glory'.[98] The Supper facilitated such an experience as it combined both dramatic and didactic elements that appealed, not only to the heart and mind, but to all the senses so, that by participation, a person might apprehend a vision of the beauty of Christ.

Edwards emphasized the Supper as an act of remembrance. It was not, however, "bare" remembrance, but a means of stirring the Christian's affections. In the same way, the Supper as a covenant seal was not to be viewed as a mere legal transaction. Rather, it involved a mutual sealing between God and his people of the covenant and its attendant blessings. His view of the Supper as a form of spiritual nourishment pointed to its richer significance as a person participated in the benefits obtained by Christ in

[96]Sweeney, *Edwards the Exegete*, 97.

[97]*WJE* 8:158.

[98]*WJE* 17:413.

his death. Yet, no one could participate in those benefits around the table who had not first experienced the reality of the converting work of the Holy Spirit in their soul.

While these aspects of the Supper offer us important insights into his understanding of the Supper its full spiritual significance is found in his view of the ordinance as a means of real communion. It was at the table that a person enjoyed a particular relationship with Christ, experiencing the fullness of the happiness that Christ had purchased by his death. For Edwards 'the sum of all that Christ purchased is the Holy Ghost. God is he of whom the purchase is made, God is the purchase and the price, and God is the thing purchased: God is the Alpha and the Omega in this work. The great thing purchased by Jesus Christ for us is communion with God, which is only in having the Spirit; 'tis participation of Christ's fullness, and having grace for grace, which is only in having of that Spirit which he has without measure; this is the promise of the Father.'[99] In the Supper, the Spirit enriched the participant's fellowship with Christ and with others. We turn to consider this in the next chapter.

[99] *WJE* 13:466.

Chapter Three
Communing with Christ and Others

The Reformers were keen to ensure that the idea of the Mass was firmly rejected; the bread and wine were not transformed into Christ's physical body and blood. Yet, the question remained about how Christ was present at the sacrament. In the Reformed tradition Zwingli rejected the idea of Christ's bodily presence, as attested both by the Mass and Luther. Nonetheless, he believed that Christ was present in his divinity at the celebration of the Supper. Calvin too eschewed the idea of Christ's bodily presence at the Supper noting that, 'The presence of Christ in the Supper we must hold to be such as neither affixes him to the element of bread, nor encloses him in bread, nor circumscribes him in any way.' Nonetheless he stated, 'I willingly admit anything which helps to express the true and substantial communication of the body and blood of the Lord, as exhibited to believers under the sacred symbols of the Supper, understanding that they are received not by the imagination or intellect merely, but are enjoyed in reality as the food of eternal life.'[1] Calvin made no attempt to explain how Christ was present in the Supper, other than to state that it was by 'the secret operation of the Spirit, which unites Christ himself to us.[2] In this way there was true communication between Christ and the believer in the sacrament.

Following in Calvin's footsteps the 1560 Scots Confession, which was composed under the supervision of John Knox who had spent time in Geneva, stated in forthright language 'we utterly condemn the vanity of those who affirm the Sacraments to be nothing else but naked and bare signs... in the

[1] Calvin, *Institutes,* IV. xvii.19.

[2] Calvin, *Institutes,* IV. xvii.31.

Supper rightly used, Christ Jesus is so joined with us, that he becomes the very nourishment and food of our souls.'[3] *The Westminster Larger Catechism* reaffirmed this approach, reflecting the mainstream of the English Puritan tradition. Question 170 asked *How do they that worthily communicate in the Lord's supper feed upon the body and blood of Christ therein?* The answer to this question was

> As the body and blood of Christ are not corporally or carnally present in, with, or under the bread and wine in the Lord's supper, and yet are spiritually present to the faith of the receiver, no less truly and really than the elements themselves are to their outward senses; so they that worthily communicate in the sacrament of the Lord's supper, do therein feed upon the body and blood of Christ, not after a corporal and carnal, but in a spiritual manner; yet truly and really, while by faith they receive and apply unto themselves Christ crucified, and all the benefits of his death.

The Savoy Declaration used similar vocabulary yet John Owen, one of its authors, admitted that, despite such assertions, how Christians received Christ in the Supper remained 'a great mystery, and great wisdom and exercise of faith lie in it.'[4] As he explored this mystery, he said that Christ offered himself in a distinct way. In the gospel God offered his Son but, in the ordinance, Christ offered himself 'making an immediate tender of himself unto a believing soul.' As he did so, he was in a sense offering 'a new and fresh sacrifice in the great work of reconciling.'[5] In the Supper there was 'a special exhibition of Jesus Christ; and it is given directly for this special exercise of faith, that we may know how to receive him in this ordinance.'[6] While Owen said that Christ offered himself in a special way, he also emphasised, like his Puritan predecessors, the necessity of the believer being in the right spiritual frame to receive him and accept his finished work of atonement. Communion involved both Christ offering himself and his right reception by the communicants. Christ did not so communicate himself

[3] Cochrane, *Reformed Confessions*, 179.

[4] Payne, *Owen Lord's Supper*, 155.

[5] Payne, *Owen Lord's Supper*, 156.

[6] Payne, *Owen Lord's Supper*, 157.

at the Supper that he was inherently present at the table. As Owen remarked 'there is an *instituted preparation* as well as a *personal disposition*.'[7]

Thomas Watson also saw Christ as present in a particular way at the Supper and posed the question 'why should faith carry away more from Christ in the Sacrament than any other grace?' He answered that faith was the most receptive and humble grace and as such it was at work in the sacrament.[8] It was also necessary to approach the Supper with prayer, asking that 'God would enrich His ordinance with His presence; that He would make the Sacrament effectual to all those holy ends and purposes for which He has appointed it.'[9] Matthew Henry stated that the Supper was a communicating ordinance in which 'Gospel benefits [are] offer'd to us, and accepted by us.'[10] Here 'humble and penitent believers partake of the blessed fruits of Christ's death; His body and blood are their food, their physick, their cordial, their life, their all. All the riches of the gospel are virtually in them.'[11] Yet, the communicant only received these benefits if they 'answer the intention of the ordinance in receiving the bread and wine, [and] we accept the offer that is made us.'[12] For both Watson and Henry, Christ was present at the sacrament, but he must also be sought in it. Neither tried to explain the sense in which Christ was present. Christ's presence, it appears, was largely assumed from the late seventeenth century onwards.

In New England, the great concern in the seventeenth century was less the contemplation of what occurred at the Supper, than its right administration, and that those who participated should be worthy to do so. Regarding what happened at the Supper, Holifield says that most 'Congregationalists assumed that the Lord's Supper offered the faithful believer the real spiritual body and blood of Christ.'[13] This is reflected in John Cotton's prayer of institution for God 'to vouchsafe his gracious presence, and the effectual working of his Spirit in us; and so to sanctify these elements both of bread and wine, and to bless his own ordinance, that we may receive by faith the

[7]Payne, *Owen Lord's Supper*, 130.

[8]Watson, *The Holy Eucharist*, 65.

[9]Watson, *The Holy Eucharist*, 74.

[10]Henry, *Communicant's Companion*, 36.

[11]Henry *Communicant's Companion*, 27.

[12]Henry, *Communicant's Companion*, 28.

[13]Holifield, "Sacramental Theology in America", 384.

body and blood of Jesus Christ, crucified for us.'[14] Stoddard's approach to the Supper not only challenged the traditional New England understanding about *who* should participate in the Supper, it also raised questions about *what* took place in the Supper. Part of Stoddard's rationale for viewing the Supper as a converting ordinance was to argue that 'All Ordinances are for the Saving good of those that they are to be administered unto. This Ordinance is according to Institution to be applyed to visible Saints, though Unconverted, therefore it is for their Saving good, and consequently for their Conversion.'[15] If all ordinances were appointed as a means of salvation, then that included the Lord's Supper. If people were excluded from the Supper, then it appeared that it had been placed above the other ordinances. Stoddard argued that this was the view that some in New England had adopted. His suggestion placed the Supper on a par with the other 'means' so that Christ could be encountered equally in any of these ordinances. In doing so, he played down the idea that the Supper provided a distinctive means of communion between Christ and the believer. As Holifield comments 'Stoddard's critics asserted the uniqueness of the Lord's Supper, while Stoddard himself affirmed the conventional Reformed doctrine that the sacrament was simply a visible Word.'[16]

Edwards stressed that the Supper was a means of real communion between Christ and the believer and at its celebration, 'There is a special presence of Christ.'[17] In a 1741 sermon on Mark 14:3 he stated 'When a Christian partakes of the Lord's Supper in a spiritual manner, then Christ always sits at the table. So, he was at the table in the first sacrament that ever was. And so it is still: whenever the believer does in a spiritual manner {partake of the Lord's Supper, Christ sits there at the table}.'[18] Danaher writes that throughout his life Edwards maintained 'that the spiritual presence of Christ, personal but not corporeal manifested itself in this ordinance.'[19] That Christ was present at the Supper established real communion with him, which was a frequent theme for Edwards as he discussed the sacrament. As McClymond and McDermott state one of the ways in which he 'put com-

[14]Quoted in Spinks, *In Remembrance*, 304.

[15]Stoddard, *Appeal to the Learned*, 25.

[16]Holifield, *The Covenant Sealed*, 214, 215.

[17]No. 668. Matthew 9:15 (b), *WJEO* 59.

[18]*WJE* 22:390.

[19]Danaher, "By Sensible Signs", 262.

munion in the foreground was by repeatedly stressing the real presence of Christ at the Lord's Table.'[20]

Communion with Christ

In a sermon from his early ministry Edwards dealt with the text 1 Corinthians 10:16, 'The cup of blessing which we bless, is it not the communion of the blood of Christ? The bread which we break, is it not the communion of the body of Christ?'[21] The sermon focused on the nature of the communion held with Christ in the ordinance. It opened with, what was for Edwards, a comparatively lengthy treatment of the context in which Paul wrote, notably eating food that had been offered to idols. For the apostle eating food that had been offered as part of idol worship was 'a visible Joining to in the worship of Idols.' It was the equivalent of 'the Holy Supper of the Christians & the Mosaic sacrifices of the Israelites & the Heathens.' Just as those who ate food offered to idols 'had visible Communion or fellowship in the worship of devils... eating & drinking together at the Lord's Table they were all looked upon [as having] Communion or to be Partakers in the worship of Christ.' Following this exposition, Edwards stated the doctrine, 'The thing designed in the sacrament of the Lord's supper is the Communion of Christians in the body & blood of Christ.'

He then examined what it meant to have communion in the body and blood of Christ. In the first instance, he made clear this was not participation in the 'proper' sense i.e., this was not a participation in the literal body and blood of Christ as in the Mass. Rather, it was 'Partaking of the benefits that are Procured by Christ's body & blood.' These benefits were well represented by food and drink because, just as these nourished the body, so Christ's benefits nourished the soul. The benefits were received 'by faith in that body & blood or in that sacrifice [and] Receiving of it & applying it to ourselves.' The other means of participation was by 'our having blessedness in the Person of Christ.' Christ died to procure happiness for his people, which consisted in 'having our souls united to his Person in beholding his excellencies & Glory and in the Enjoyment of his Love in having spiritual Conversation with him in this world and in Enjoying of him in the world.' As we saw in the previous chapter, the Supper was a place where a person experienced the happiness of abiding in Christ's love.

[20]McClymond and McDermott, *Theology of Jonathan Edwards*, 490.

[21]No. 156. 1 Corinthians 10:16(a), *WJEO* 45.

He then considered how Christians had communion with Christ in the Supper writing 'they not only have Communion in him but they have Communion with him. They not only Partake of him but they are Joint Partakers with him.' This was because when Christ invites his people to eat and drink 'he sits with them at the Table' and, in doing so, 'Partakes with his People' of the benefits of his own body & blood [and] of his own sacrifice & Righteousness.' Edwards developed this idea by noting that Jesus, by his death, obtained justification 'having suffered Enough to answer the Imputed Guilt that Lay upon him' and, as a result, justified sinners have fellowship with Christ in his own body and blood. He then turned his attention to the inaugural Lord's Supper which Christ celebrated with his disciples remarking, 'so he doth still Partake with his Church in the spiritual benefits signified in the Lord Supper.' Christ's bodily presence at the first Supper was a sign that he would evermore be present at the Supper. Those who attended the ordinance in the proper manner 'may look upon him as sitting with them at his Table.' Communion was not simply a personal communion between Christ and the believer, it was also a corporate experience in which Christians communicated with the local church, the universal church, and the church triumphant.

Despite seeing communion as transcending the boundaries of time and space Edwards explained that it was 'by sensible signs Represented.' He recognised that there was something mundane in this act of eating and drinking. Indeed, the use of such basic commodities as bread and wine was designed to avoid any ceremonial pomp. Instead, this simple meal 'Represented Christ offering himself up [as] a sacrifice for us in the bruising of his body & spilling his blood.' Such ordinary elements could never fully represent all that Christ had suffered in his death, but they gave the participant a partial insight into it. In this way the breaking of the bread 'signifies the Greatness & extremity of his sufferings [as] he was as it were broken in Pieces for us.' Furthermore, the one who ministered the sacrament 'stands in Christ's stead & Represents him. He Gives the sacramental Elements to the People in the name of Christ.' While the Supper represented what Christ had done in his death, it also represented his people as they 'accept Christ's offer of himself & benefits.' It is then by faith that believers 'Come to have actual communion in the body & blood of Christ' and show that they have found their blessedness in that body and blood.

For Edwards there was real communion with Christ in the Supper. The participation in the body and blood of Christ was not in terms of benefiting from its physical properties but through enjoying the benefits obtained by

Christ's death. These were received by faith as the communicant sat with Christ at his table. Christ's presence at the table was indicated by the fact that he enjoyed the benefits of his own death, had indicated his ongoing presence by his participation in the original Supper, and was now represented by the minister who stood in his place.

Edwards preached on this text again in August 1745.[22] While this sermon was different from the earlier one, it again focused on the theme of communion. He began by pointing out that the word communion came from the Latin word *communio,* which was a translation of the Greek word *koine,* and meant fellowship. He offered several New Testament examples of how this term was used, such as when it described fellowship in the gospel. He followed this by an investigation of 'What is meant by the communion of the body & blood of Christ?' He answered that such communion 'meant a feast or a common partaking & Enjoying.' In this feast, he noted, communicants partook of the body and blood of Christ, although not in a physical sense. With this caveat in place, Edwards argued that the Supper was nonetheless a physical event as 'There is a sensible Representation of this Communion and Joint partaking of the body & Blood.' The bread and the wine were signs, just as words too were signs, pointing to another reality. The bread and wine, however, were signs of a different order because God has appointed these 'to be perceived also by our other senses.'

He again drew attention to the nature of the Supper as a dramatic re-enactment of the first Lord's Supper as he noted, 'Here is a Representation Of almost every thing that belongs to the first Communion.' Edwards then enumerated the ways in which the Supper reflected its first celebration as the minister stood in Christ's place, the bread and wine represented the body and blood, the suffering of Christ and his offering himself to God and to believers as they fed upon the elements. He continued that in participating in the Supper 'True Believers hence [experience] Communion as a Joint Participation by Receiving by Faith.' Once more he placed particular emphasis upon the physical nature of this. For as the believer reached out his hand, and received the food at the table, he did so by faith and received refreshment, enjoyment, nourishment, strength, and comfort. The food and drink provided demonstrated to the believer the benefits of their salvation and their 'union with Christ by which they have Communion.' The Supper engaged both the senses and the imagination, which distinguished it from other ordinances.

[22]No. 791. 1 Corinthians 10:16(b), *WJEO* 63.

He then explored the nature of this communion by pointing out that it meant three things. In the first instance, the Supper was instructive in the way that God's word was instructive. It was instructive as it fixed the participants' contemplation and affected their hearts by recalling 'the desireableness *of* the Benefits' of Christ. Secondly, communion with Christ sealed the covenant of grace on behalf of both parties. Christ sealed the covenant with his blood, while believers renewed their oath, which he noted was the original meaning of the term sacrament. Thirdly, communion occurred as God gave his 'special Bles[sing]' to the means that he had appointed. He added that this is 'God's appointed way wherein it is his Revealed will that He will bestow this Benefit.'

Edwards then went on to say that great events have great memorials and this Supper ordained by God was a fitting memorial to the greatest event in history. The reason that it was so appropriate was its simplicity. The fact that this was a plain meal meant that the mind was not drawn off to consider the splendour of the memorial but focused a person's contemplation on the reality to which it pointed. He continued, that it was also appropriate because it was a 'lively representation' of the spiritual benefits of Christ's nourishment. Twice he described the Supper as lively, three times as affecting and once as both lively and affecting. As a result, Christ's benefits were not only represented in the Supper, 'but given sweet union and communion', as when a king invites his subject to a feast.

This led him to remark 'How great is the wickedness of such as live in the careless neglect of this ordinance.' He added that it was necessary for the church to remove from its midst those who lived visibly scandalous lives for 'such Persons might not sit down with others at this Holy ordinance.' This was especially important given that the Supper was a 'manifestation of our union with Christ. Love to him. Gratitude of our Receiving him [and] giving up our selves to him.' To admit a person to the Supper who was visibly scandalous and impenitent was to mock the visible meaning of the sacrament as the 'Christians Communion with Christ' and 'union one to another as members of the same Special Family & the same Mystical Body of Christ.' This communion occurred in the Supper because of 'Their being actually the subjects of [the] Benefits of his body & blood.' Since Christ was present at the table, their eating and drinking meant there was 'Joint Participation itself with Christ.' This sense of participation with Christ was further enhanced since it involved 'Him that ministers in his name' and who acts, therefore, as Christ's representative at the Supper. In this way the

Supper brings Christ into contemplation by both 'instructing the mind & affecting the Heart.'

While there is much common ground between the two sermons this latter section from the 1745 sermon perhaps reveals how Edwards' understanding of the Supper was now brought before the public in a more explicit manner. There was particular emphasis upon the exclusion from the Supper of those who lived scandalous lives. While this was not unusual for Edwards, or at odds with the practice of Solomon Stoddard, the rationale offered for this exclusion was striking. He was clear that those who were unrepentant and admitted to the Supper were not beneficiaries of Christ's work, therefore they could not truly participate in a meal which celebrated that work, and at which Christ himself was present to communicate with his people. If none could benefit from the Supper except those who enjoy a true relationship with Christ, then this struck at the heart of his grandfather's vision of the sacrament as a converting ordinance. Here was an early public indication of Edwards' change of stance which he elsewhere dated as occurring around this time.

While hinting at what was to come it did not mark a departure from his understanding of the Lord's Supper as expressed from the earliest days of his ministry. In a sacrament sermon, dating from 1729, based on Song of Solomon 5:1, 'Eat, O friends; drink, yea, drink abundantly, O beloved' Edwards explored the nature of the communion experienced at the Lord's Table.[23] In typical Puritan fashion, Edwards viewed Song of Solomon, or Canticles as it then known, as speaking about the relationship between Christ as the bridegroom, and his church as the bride. He understood this statement in chapter 5 as Christ responding to the prayer of his church when they asked for the Holy Spirit to 'Come and breath his Gracious Influence upon the heart of the spouse to Cause her Graces to flow and to be in a vigorous Exercise that it might be the more fitted for Christ's Presence and Enjoyment.' In the text Christ replied to the prayer of the church by inviting it to feast upon his love and graces. Edwards observed this invitation was to 'the same Church which is his beloved, is made up of believers that are his friends' and who were 'Invited to Eat and Drink [these] benefits [and] to Partake of spiritual delights & satisfy their spiritual appetites.' He told the congregation they were to lay no restraint upon their appetites but to drink and be drunk, stating his doctrine as 'That Persons need not and ought not to set any bounds to their spiritual & Gracious Appetites.'

[23]No. 117. Canticles 5:1, *WJEO* 44

He explained that humanity had been created with two different sets of appetites, which were the natural, or animal appetites, and the holy or spiritual appetites. With the Fall, the spiritual appetites had been subjected to the natural appetites but, through regeneration, the spiritual appetites had now been renewed, at least in part. Since this was only a partial restoration, the physical appetites now needed to be restrained through their mortification. Yet, while the physical appetites should be controlled, no such limits should be set on the spiritual appetites, which ought to be given 'Unbounded liberty.' Such spiritual appetites were the consequence of being 'truly born again.' As Danaher writes 'the imparting of a "spiritual appetite" provided the basis on which the faculties of reason, affection and will recaptured their prelapsarian sense of proportion.'[24]

Edwards then combined several biblical images to describe how those who were regenerated now experienced a new hunger and thirst. They were now like Christ, whose meat and drink were to do the will of the Father. They were like the Psalmist who longed for God as the hart panted for the stream. They had an appetite for Christ who was the bread come down from heaven. In particular, they longed for the word of God, as they no longer lived by bread alone, but hungered for the nourishment of the word, as a baby longs for his mother's milk. He continued that this desire arose not only 'from a Rational Consideration of the need & benefit of it but 'tis a desire Immediately flowing from His new nature like the natural appetite.' This language offers an echo of an important idea for Edwards that the regenerate person has a new spiritual sense or sense of the heart, which is not available to the unregenerate. As Michael McClymond summarises this understanding of the new sense, 'He insisted on God's immediate presence to each believer and on the indispensability of divine grace. Yet simultaneously he asserted that the spiritual sense was a kind of evidence for God's reality and that the perception of God's beauty and truth enabled the human mind to perceive truth and beauty wherever it appears.[25]

Edwards urged his congregation to indulge their new spiritual appetite, and to do so, in ways that functioned as a counterpoint to their base appetites. As the covetous, the ambitious and the sensual pursued their earthy desires, so the regenerate should pursue 'those Pleasures that are spiritual, the Pleasure of seeing the Glory of Christ and Enjoying his love and having Communion with him.' He again exhorted them to remember the indulgence

[24]Danaher, "By Sensible Signs", 270.

[25]McClymond, "Spiritual Perception", 197.

of such spiritual appetites should be without boundaries, noting that 'there is no such thing as any Inordinateness in holy affections.' Furthermore, he added, 'there Cannot be a too frequent or too Powerfull exercise of them.'

Since these new spiritual appetites, unlike physical appetites, have no boundaries, then Christians should seek to inflame them and indulge them as they are 'the highest perfection of our nature.' It is in the indulgence of such appetites that people would find the happiness for which God has created them. God had not only made them for this happiness but had also given them voracious spiritual appetites which could never exceed his provision for them. He told his congregation that 'our hungerings & thirstings after God & Jesus Christ & after holiness Can't be too Great for the nature of the things, for they are things of Infinite value.' With this in view, Edwards called on his congregation 'to Promote a thirsting desire after Jesus Christ and after that Glorious feast of spiritual Good things that is provided in him.' As we have already seen in Chapter 2, these themes are typical of Edwards' theology that God has made humanity for happiness which consists in knowing God, and therefore a person should do everything to obtain that happiness.

In order both to satisfy these renewed spiritual appetites, and to stimulate them, Edwards pleaded with his listeners to avoid carnal temptations, which only satisfied the lower nature, and to place themselves in the way of all 'allurement' and 'enticement' to every opportunity to indulge their spiritual appetites. This meant they should often be in prayer and frequently give themselves to reading and hearing the word. In particular, he noted 'to this End we ought to Carefully & with the utmost seriousness & Consideration attend the sacrament of the Lord's Supper.' This was because the Supper was given especially to draw the believer's heart towards Christ and to increase a sense of longing for him. It was also in the Supper that these longings were satisfied by the 'visible signs' which set Christ crucified before his people. Spiritual meat and drink were displayed here before participants, which excited their spiritual hunger and thirst, since they saw represented the spiritual feast that God had provided for them in Christ, and which satisfied their souls. Indeed, he declared 'here we may hope in some measure to have our Longing souls satisfied in this world by the Gracious Communications of the spirit of God.' As this final comment makes clear, Edwards saw in the celebration of the Supper a deeper form of communion with Christ than that which was afforded by the other ordinances.

Such an experience of communion was only available to those who had were indwelt by the Holy Spirit. No-one could profit in such a way from coming to the table without such a prior experience. Edwards saw human behaviour as governed by disposition or habit. This disposition was 'a law that God has fixed, that such actions upon such occasions should be exerted.'[26] An unregenerate person would act in accordance with their fallen nature, while a regenerate person would act in harmony with their new spiritual disposition as the Holy Spirit became 'an indwelling vital principle.'[27] As a result of 'the exercise of this divine disposition, a person was changed and ultimately renewed after the image of God.'[28] The Supper provided just such an opportunity for the exercise of this disposition through the stimulation of the spiritual appetites. As Edwards stated in a sacramental sermon on 2 Corinthians 3:18 'believers have such a sight of the Glory of Christ as Revealed in the Gospel as Changes 'em into a likeness to the same Glory.'[29] He offered no hint that the Supper would create appetites in the unconverted or that it would stir up appetites they did not possess. Indeed, he warned that the person who sought Christ in the performance of religious duties did not realise that he was 'as far from a principle of holiness as ever, that his nature is as Contrary to God as ever, his heart is opposite to the Gospel as ever.'

One of the reasons that the communion Christians enjoyed at the Supper offered satisfaction was because of its eschatological dimensions. For Edwards, looking back, the Passover had been a type of the Supper that was now fulfilled in Christ.[30] Looking forward it was an anticipation of the great eschatological feast. The idea of the feast in heaven was a familiar theme for him as he sought to describe the final happiness of the believer. In *Miscellanies No. 1274* he quoted favourably the words of the English Puritan Thomas Goodwin that,

> Sitting together in heavenly places in Christ implies first the pleasures of that kingdom... Now it is familiar in the Old Testament, and in the New, [...] to express the pleasures of heaven by sitting at a table, to banquet it with the great king that maketh that feast... for we shall sit in heaven then, and enjoy this new wine, which is the Holy Ghost filling us with the Godhead, that

[26] *WJE* 13:358.

[27] *WJE* 8:67.

[28] Luke, "Disposition", 148.

[29] No. 72. 2 Corinthians 3:18, *WJEO* 43.

[30] No. 294. 1 Corinthians 5:7, *WJEO* 48.

> is, filling us with the pleasures and blessedness that is in God himself.[31]

In an installation sermon preached in 1746 on Isaiah 62:4, 5 he described the glorification of the church as that time when 'She shall then be brought to the entertainments of an eternal wedding feast, and to dwell eternally with her bridegroom; yea to dwell eternally in his embraces. Then Christ will give her his love; and she shall drink her fill, yea she shall swim in the ocean of his love.'[32] The Supper was a shadow and foretaste of the great feast that Christians would enjoy with Christ and with each other in glory. As Bezzant writes for Edwards 'the Supper exercises a proleptic function'[33] that anticipated the full blessings of the eschaton.

Edwards explored the eschatological dimension of the Supper in a 1733 sermon on Luke 22:30, 'That ye may eat and drink at my table in my kingdom.'[34] Here he linked the Last Supper with the ongoing celebration of the sacrament, and its anticipation of the great feast to come. He stated that the Last Supper was the 'first sacrament of the supper', where Christ took the opportunity to speak to his disciples 'of another Table of his at which he Promises that his disciples shall Eat & drink hereafter in his Kingdom.' The fact that Christ had served them at the table was a reminder to them of the 'Honour which he designed for them hereafter' when they 'should Eat & drink at his Table in Glory.'

At the Last Supper Christ told his disciples that there were two aspects to this kingdom 'or Rather the same Kingdom in different Respects.' There was the kingdom that the Father promised to him, and there was the kingdom that he promised to them. The kingdom that the Father gives to Christ was, in fact, the same one in which he invited his disciples to share. Christ could then say to them, 'I appoint unto you a Kingdom... that ye may Eat & drink at my Table in my Kingdom.' He continued to point out that in this kingdom they would feast like kings, and 'Eat & drink that which is most dainty.' Christ told them, 'as ye have Just now Eat & drink at my sacramental Table here on Earth with me in my state of humiliation, So shall ye feast with me in my state of Exaltation.'

[31] *WJE* 23:220.

[32] *WJE* 25:182.

[33] Bezzant, "Ecclesiology and Sacraments', 274.

[34] No. 287. Luke 22:30, *WJEO* 48.

Edwards stated his doctrine as 'The saints shall hereafter as it were Eat & drink with Christ at his Table [in] His Kingdom of Glory.' He explained how in both Testaments the blessings of the kingdom of God were spoken of in terms of feasting, while 'the blessings of the Gospel that believers do partake of while in this world they are but Earnests of those future benefits that shall be bestowed upon them.'[35] Those future benefits, however, were so glorious that they could not be imagined, therefore God 'makes use of many similitudes to Represent it to our minds.' Christ had now entered glory, and ultimately his people 'Shall be Present with him in the highest sense & most Immediate. This is Intimated in their Eating and drinking with him at his Table.' On that day, his people shall see him face to face and he shall be able 'Immediately to Converse with them as persons that Eat together at the same Table.'

Since this meal was a foretaste of the eschatological reward that Christians will experience when 'the saints fully Enjoy Christ and shall with Christ Enjoy G[od] the F[ather and] shall partake with him in his Enjoym[en]t of the F[ather's] Love & the Complacence that he hath in his son', they 'should Prize and Improve the sacrament of the Lord's Supper.' As they took part in the Supper, they should remember that Christ appointed it to represent 'the assembly of the blessed sitting Eating in Communion with Christ in Heaven.' Furthermore, diligent partaking of the Supper also prepared the Christian for the 'glorious communion' that was to come. The Lord's Supper ought to be viewed as a 'foretaste of that Eternal feast with Christ in Glory' and it is 'a foretaste and Earnest of that future Happiness.' Notably, he remarked that this can only be a foretaste 'Given to the worthy Partakers.' Clearly, those who were not true believers could not enjoy in the Supper a foretaste of something for which they have not received an earnest and to which they had no right. Christians, he warned, should be careful how they attended the sacrament and not do so in a 'heinous manner', since it represented 'the assembly of the blessed in Communion with Christ in Heaven.' For Edwards, those who showed contempt for the Supper on earth also showed contempt for the feast in heaven. He further warned the ungodly, not because of their neglect or abuse of the table, but for their failure to embrace the happiness that was offered to them in the gospel. He urged them to seek salvation, otherwise they would have no entrance to the eternal feast.

Another dimension of communion explored by Edwards was that the believer not only enjoyed receiving from Christ in the sacrament, but also

[35] An earnest was an older English term for a deposit or down payment.

gave to him. The Supper was not simply an occasion for the believer to receive grace, but in its celebration, there was mutual giving and receiving in communion. He highlighted this in a 1741 sermon preached on Mary's anointing of Christ in Mark 14. He saw this act as a picture of the Christian's wholehearted sacrifice and commitment to Christ. He made clear that such an act was of no benefit to Christ, he nonetheless accepted it as an offering of pure devotion. While this was a not a sacramental sermon[36] Edwards made the point that this act of devotion took place at a meal, and he drew a parallel with the Lord's Supper, where 'the believer does as it were feast with Christ. He is fed with that food that Christ has prepared for his people at great cost' and that 'Christ himself sits at the table with the believer at such a time.' Again, for Edwards the parallel was with the Last Supper and as Christ was present then, he was now present at the sacrament as he 'partakes of the Lord's Supper in a spiritual manner.'[37]

He then explained that since Christ was present at the table now the worthy participant ministered to Christ in the same manner as Mary. He stated that 'at such times the heart is purified, and the exercises of divine love flow out of a broken heart like precious perfumed ointment upon Christ, the head of the church.' Again, this echoes Edwards' view of the eschatological feast where there is a mutual giving and receiving. In his sermon on Isaiah 62:4, 5, he stated that at the eternal consummation while 'Christ brings [the church] to eat and drink at his own table, to take her fill of his own entertainments... yet he, on the other hand, has fellowship with her; he feasts with her; her joys are his; and he rejoices in that entertainment that she provides for him.'[38] At the Supper a Christian not only received from Christ and ministered to him but also 'towards others that are his fellow members, even towards the least and meanest of them, towards not only the head but the feet.' In ministering to other believers, the Christian demonstrated that 'the heart is devoted and offered up in sacrifice to Christ.'[39] Communion with Christ necessarily included communion with other believers.

While Edwards placed great emphasis upon actual communion with Christ in the Supper, he was clear that this did not occur as a matter of course. Christ was not automatically present at its celebration. Christians

[36]*WJE* 22:379. Stout comments in his introduction 'this sermon may have been preached for a "contribution," an occasion on which the pastor asks for charitable donations for some cause.'

[37]*WJE* 22:390.

[38]*WJE* 25:181.

[39]*WJE* 22:390.

could celebrate the Supper and find that Christ was absent. As he had warned his congregation in an early sermon 'it will be a sorrowfull thing if we Come to ordinances & see nothing of Christ in them.' It was necessary, therefore, when coming to the Supper to 'wait upon G[od] by his spirit to Give us to see the beauty of & the divine excellency of his dying Love.'[40]

In the sacrament sermon preached in 1742 on Matthew 9:15 Edwards spoke about the need to seek to enjoy the fulness of Christ's presence. By this time, he was concerned that the town of Northampton had once again fallen into spiritual decay after the revival had passed. Something of his unease is evident in the sermon as he warned them that spiritual lethargy had an impact on their celebration of the Supper. After briefly opening the text he stated his doctrine as 'when a Company or society of Christians have Christ present with them tis the greatest cause of Joy to them.'[41] He developed the doctrine by remarking that there was a 'degree of Christ's gracious presence that true Christians alwaies have. After a soul is converted Christ never whol[ly] leaves it. He has promised that he will never leave them nor forsake them.' This bond between Christ and the believer was primarily through the presence of his indwelling Spirit. This exceeded the physical presence that Christ's disciples experienced during his time on earth. While Christ in this sense was always with his people there was, however, a further means in which believers might enjoy his presence which went beyond this. Edwards described this as the 'Presence of Christ by special manifestation of himself. & tokens of his presence whereby Christ at some times may be said to be Present with Christians and not at others.' He then reminded his listeners that 'we a little while ago had the bridegroom with us in a very remarkable & wonderful manner manifesting his beauty & Glory, shewing us his Love & kindness. We were then a company so secured as is spoken of in the doctrine.' He added, rather soberly, 'but to how great a degree has Christ withdrawn from us.' Although, remembering that Christ had promised never to leave his people or forsake them, he added, 'I would hope that [we] are not wholly without manifestations of the presence of Christ yet tis in no measure as it has been but we have declined & grown dull & dead.' Christ's presence with the town, he continued, was now like his earthly presence with the Pharisees, where he was beside them but not with them in his special, gracious presence. There was now a need for the

[40]No. 72. 2 Corinthians 3:18(a), *WJEO* 42.

[41]No. 668. Matthew 9:15(b), *WJEO* 59.

people of Northampton to mourn the absence of Christ's special presence, to humble themselves and to earnestly seek that presence once more.

This withdrawal of Christ's special presence was particularly significant in their celebration of the Lord's Supper and, he told them, there was a need to seek his presence at the sacrament once more. This sense of Christ's absence was noticeable at the Supper because, as he pointed out, it was there they 'especially appear as the Children of the bride chamber. We come to present our selves in the Bride chamber at a feast that Christ has provided for us there.' If Christ is present at that meal, then 'it will make that feast Joyfull to us above all things in the [world].' If, however, 'we come to the Lord's supper & find nothing of Christ there & don't meet with him we shall [have] reason to go away mourning & with heavy hearts.' Since this was the case, Edwards exhorted his congregation to remove all sinful hindrances and engage in all Christian exercises so that they might once again enjoy the special sense of Christ's presence, at the Supper.

Once more it is clear from Edwards' comments that he viewed Christ as being present at the Supper in a distinctive way which offered real communion with him. Yet, while he was present at the Supper he could also be driven from his own table and there was a need, therefore, 'earnestly to seek the return of the presence of Christ amongst us.' These comments were clearly directed to those whose recently intensified spiritual affections had now abated.

Communion with Others

One aspect of the Supper that the Reformers had sought to recover was its communal dimension. The Supper was an expression not only of communion between Christ and his church, but of fellowship between believers. It was part of a significant move away from the medieval sacramental view which saw the participants as recipients of grace through the ministrations of the Church. There was now an emphasis upon communion as a shared meal and not a performance. As Hughes Oliphant Old notes 'The sign Jesus gave was the sharing of a meal and as the Reformers understood it the visual sign should look like a meal shared by the communicants.' How this was reflected visually varied from place to place as efforts were made to 'make the celebration look more like sharing a meal.'[42] For example, in some settings, those who participated in the meal sat together around a table to emphasise

[42] Old, *Holy* Communion, 32.

the commonality of their experience. Notably, the altar was replaced by a table or, in some instances, several tables. In New England the congregation received the bread and wine as they remained seated and were served by deacons.[43] This tradition of the Supper as a communal meal was inherited by Edwards and, as Bezzant observes, 'Like his Puritan forebears, Edwards understood ministry as a conscious repudiation of sacramentally centered Roman Catholicism and a kind of Protestantism that gave significant space to lay piety and ministrations.'[44] He too laid a strong emphasis upon the communal aspects of celebrating the sacrament.

Hunt has pointed out that such was the emphasis on the communal dimension of the Supper that in the English Reformed tradition 'One aspect of the sacrament that was firmly rooted in popular culture was its function as an instrument of reconciliation.' For example, he quotes the Puritan minister Jeremiah Dyke who stated 'This is a truth confessed on all hands that men should bee in charity that come to the Sacrament.'[45] Likewise, William Ames wrote that having a point of contention with one's neighbour ought not to cause a person to abstain from the sacrament 'but rather to lay it down speedily that he may communicate.'[46] There was a similar emphasis in Scotland where 'The 'day of reconciliation' regularly appears in the schedules set up for communion seasons, along with 'exhorting the whole of the neighbourhood to mutual peace and love.'[47]

In New England, despite following in this tradition, there was, it seems, less focus upon the Supper as a means of reconciliation. This may have been due to the prolonged debate over who had the right to receive the Supper which encouraged introspection in search of a true work of grace, rather than examining relationships with one's neighbours. Certainly, by the time Edwards arrived in Northampton there was little evidence that the Lord's Supper, or indeed any other means, had encouraged reconciliation in the town. Alan Strange remarks, when he became pastor 'the ungodly behavior of the youth and various feuding families caused him to question the sincerity and spiritual health of many Northampton parishioners.'[48] For Edwards the divisions in the town would have been a particular issue when it came to

[43]Davies, *American Puritans*, 166.

[44]Bezzant, *Jonathan Edwards and the Church*, 111.

[45]Hunt, "The Lord's Supper", 47, 48.

[46]Ames, *Conscience*, Book IV, 84.

[47]Todd, *Culture of Protestantism*, 92.

[48]Strange, "Edwards on Visible Sainthood", 119.

the celebration of the sacrament, as he reflected the older view which saw the Supper as the occasion for reconciliation between communicants.

Edwards clearly held that the Supper ought to be a meal expressing union, not only between Christ and his people, but between the people themselves. Writing in *The Blank Bible* about the problems surrounding the Lord's Supper addressed by Paul in 1 Corinthians 11, he noted 'it seems that in the primitive church the Lord's Supper was made use of, partly as a feast of charity, to feed the poor, and satisfy the hungry; and by reason of their having of it so, very often it considerably answered this end.'[49] As such, the Supper represented more than the personal relationship between the communicant and Christ which historically had been it focus in New England. The meal was an expression of corporate church life and, as Edwards' made clear, this went beyond simple charity.

In a 1729 sacrament sermon on 1 Corinthians 1:9, 'God is faithful, by whom ye were called unto the fellowship of his Son Jesus Christ our Lord',[50] Edwards explained how the nature of union and communion with Christ was displayed at the Supper. He began by pointing his hearers to the eschatological dimension of the sacrament, showing that in Christ they had God's invitation, promise and earnest of the more complete fellowship with Christ that was to come. Focusing upon the second part of his text he stated the doctrine 'That we are called by the gospel to communion with Christ.'

At its most fundamental level communion, he explained, simply meant partaking in a common blessing, as a person enjoyed God's holiness and happiness. This was the shared experience of Christians and was one that they displayed at the Lord's Table as 'they there partake in common of the same body & the same blood of Christ. They Eat of the same spiritual meat and drink together of the same spiritual drink and that by their Partaking of the same Elements their Common Partaking of the same benefits of Christ's death is signified.' This was the essence of all that the New Testament meant by the term fellowship or communion. In the same way communion with the Holy Spirit was a common sharing in fellowship with him as 'they Are Partakers together with Christ and one with Another of the same spirit.' It was through common participation in the Holy Spirit that they were enabled to have fellowship with the Father, the Son and, also, with one another. It was their common enjoyment of these benefits that gave rise to a 'mutual

[49] *WJE* 24:1050.

[50] No. 103. 1 Corinthians 1:9, *WJEO* 44.

society' which 'begets love & friendship and a mutual Intercourse and this is also Intended in the meaning of the word Communion.'

Edwards explained that communion is 'not a Partaking of the same benefits separately & Ignorantly & unwillingly but 'tis a Common Partaking of benefits in union & society.' The communion Christians enjoyed was rooted in their preceding union with Christ, and they must recognise that this is the foundation of their communion with one another. He maintained that this 'Union alwaies Goes before Communion.' True communion is communion with Christ, and it necessitates communion with one another. This is a significant point regarding Edwards' understanding of the Supper, that there can be no real communion between those who participate in the sacrament that is not first rooted in their sharing the benefits of union with Christ. To underline his point Edwards stated that it was 'therefore a vulgar mistake that Communion is nothing else but only society or Conversation. To have Communion as many mistakenly Understand it is nothing else but to have spiritual Conversation with God.' It was possible for a person to sit at the table, take the bread and wine and yet not have communion with God or his people.

He then outlined, in a manner echoing John Owen, how the Christian had communion with each of the persons of the Trinity.[51] In the first instance there was communion with the Son which came, particularly, as Christians shared in Christ's righteousness. This was Christ's reward from the Father for going to cross, and as the Father was 'well Pleased with him for it so he accepts & is well pleased with believers for it also.' Christ was justified by his death on the cross, and Christians now share in this justification. Secondly, they also had communion with the Father because Christ is God's Son and 'by virtue of their Union to him they also stand in the Relation of sons.' This meant that 'they have Communion with Christ in the Father's love & delight.' They also had communion with the Holy Spirit, which Edwards described as 'the main thing' because as 'those that Are in Christ they have the spirit of Christ. Those that have not the spirit of Christ they Are none of his.' In this way, Christians participated in the grace that flowed to them from the Spirit, through Christ.

The idea that Christians have communion with each of the members of the Trinity reflects Bezzant's comment that 'The outcome of emphasis on the sociality of the Godhead is not only to provide individuals with access to this

[51]Owen, *Communion,* passim. Owen saw communion with the Father primarily in terms of enjoying his love, communion with the Son in receiving his grace and communion with the Holy Spirit in the application of Christ's work.

triune life through the indwelling Spirit but also to present the church with the opportunity of defining itself in relation to this triunity and of modeling itself to some degree on the triune life.'[52] Consequently, the society that is formed around the Lord's Table, not only participated in the life of the Trinity, it reflected the fellowship that exists within the Trinity. As Edwards continued, believers are participants in the divine nature, divine knowledge, and divine comfort before, finally, becoming participants with Christ in glory as they 'Partake of the same Glory in heaven.' He concluded that there was, therefore, a 'spiritual society between Christ and believers that is founded in their Common Partaking of benefits.' Amy Plantinga Pauw suggests this high view of the communion that saints enjoyed, and that anticipated the eschatological feast, meant that 'Edwards as pastor was repeatedly tempted by an ecclesiology of glory that sought the eschatological perfection of Christ's bride amidst the frailties of the earthly communion of saints.'[53] In truth, he was all too conversant with such frailties, and in this sermon stated, with more than a hint of realism, this communion 'many times is much Interrupted in this world and attended by darkness and by Reason of those Remains of sin & Corruption there are.' While Edwards was capable of lofty theological insights, he was always conscious of the obduracy of the human heart and the sinful weakness of Christians.

The theme of the corporate nature of the Supper was again picked up in the application where he stated that Christians 'in having Communion with Christ... have Communion one with Another.' He further developed this idea in the hortatory section of the sermon where he pointed out that as Christians participated with Christ at his table and enjoyed his benefits they did so in 'Christ's friendship & society with his People as with his family at his Table.' It was as they met in this way 'that Christ delights to meet with his People and will Give his blessing.' It is for this reason that Edwards could say his appeal was to 'a serious and Carefull & Joyfull attendance on the Lord's Supper. It was Instituted on purpose for the saints Communion. Christians Communion with Christ and one with another.' The Supper represented 'how all the Church of Christ doth together Partake with Christ in his spiritual benefits. How they Partake with him in the benefit of his suffering & Righteousness and partaking with him of his spirit and of his Joy & comfort.' This echoes the even more effusive language that he used in a sermon on 1 Corinthians 11:27 where he spoke of the Supper as the,

[52]Bezzant, *Jonathan Edwards and the Church*, 67.

[53]Pauw, "Jonathan Edwards' Ecclesiology", 178.

> representation [of the] union of Christ [and his people in a] union of hearts. [It is a] relative union, [like] a father among his children. [It is a] a marriage union: the Bridegroom manifesting his great Love and offering Himself, the Bride receiving, the vital union. Here is also Represented their union [with] one another meet[ing] together as Brethren. Chil[dren] of one Family—as one spouse of [Christ]—as all united in one Head, all having communion in the same benefits and so all united in the same interest: all united in Hearts as partakers together in the feast of mutual friendship and love.[54]

Although this sermon was preached at Stockbridge in 1751 after his dismissal, there is ample evidence in Edwards' earlier corpus that he saw the Supper as an expression of union between Christ and his church. He also knew, however, that the benefits could only be truly shared and enjoyed by those who were united to Christ.

For Edwards, the corporate aspect of the Supper was also important as an expression of the communal joy of Christian experience. For much of the preceding century the Lord's Supper had been a focus of division in New England. The emphasis that was placed upon self-examination and the danger of eating and drinking unworthily had led many people to neglect the sacrament. Stoddard's attempts to reverse this trend with his own peculiar view of the table had little effect. As Minkema notes Edwards wanted 'his listeners to appreciate the privilege and joy of the Lord's Supper, to see it not as a formal duty but as a happy event.'[55] One way of doing this was to see it as a communal event in which believers enjoyed Christ's presence in a particular way and, also, shared in the mutual enjoyment of Christ's blessings. While he did not fail to warn and admonish those who would partake of the Supper in an unworthy manner, as the next chapter will make clear, he nonetheless wanted participants to see the real value and accompanying joy that there was in meeting with Christ at the table. As Bezzant points out 'Edwards is concerned about the lack of regard for the Lord's Supper. He sees it as a means by which individuals might express their devotion and by which the community might be brought together.'[56]

[54]No. 977. 1 Corinthians 10:17(b), *WJEO* 69.

[55]Editor's Introduction, *WJE* 14:39.

[56]Bezzant, *Jonathan Edwards and the Church*, 124.

It must be remembered that most of his sacramental sermons were not preached at the celebration of the sacrament but in the week prior to its celebration on a Sunday. The aim of the sermons was to urge his listeners not to neglect the sacrament but to receive its communal benefits. It is a reminder that those who point to Edwards' neglect of ecclesiology[57] because of his emphasis on the spiritual condition of the individual have missed an important dimension of his thought. Edwards drew attention to the individual's spiritual condition, not to place them in a doubting frame of mind, but to stir the affections of his congregants by pointing them to a spiritual reality that, was evident in the communal enjoyment of the Supper and which lay beyond the social formality of church going.

That he conceived of the Supper in this way is not surprising. As we have seen he viewed the Supper as an anticipation of the eschatological feast. That feast was a momentous event, not only in terms of the Christian enjoying Christ, but also in terms of enjoying complete harmony with other saints. In his most famous description of the believer's reward, *Heaven is a World of Love*, he spoke of how for the saints, 'All their love is holy, humble, and perfectly Christian, without the least impurity or carnality; where love is always mutual, where the love of the beloved is answerable to the love of the lovers; where there is no hypocrisy or dissembling, but perfect simplicity and sincerity; where is no treachery, unfaithfulness or inconstancy, nor any such thing as jealousy.[58] In heaven all the disharmony and division that beset Northampton would be removed. Christians had a foretaste of the world that was to come when they enjoyed fellowship with one another in the celebration of the Supper.

Edwards' statements about the nature of communion between Christians reflected his essential ecclesiology. As Crisp states 'Axiomatic to Edwards' conception of the nature of the Church was the notion that the elect comprising the true Church are united with Christ as his bride, his mystical body, in some way that involves a metaphysically real union between the two.'[59] In a 1735 sermon he remarked 'this is Especially one End of the Lord's suppers that in that ordinance Christ might as it were bring his Church to him into his banqueting House & Present her to himself in sweet & holy Communion.'[60] Communion consisted of more than the merely external

[57] Bezzant, *Jonathan Edwards and the Church,* 4.

[58] *WJE* 8:385.

[59] Crisp, "Closing the Table", 58.

[60] No. 358. Ephesians 5:25–27, *WJEO* 44.

performance of the sacrament. The sacrament was deeply mystical, not only in terms of the transcendent interaction between Christ and his church, but also in the spiritual interaction between the members of the church. Notably, Edwards stated this to his congregation more than a decade before he began to work out his arguments about admission to the Supper.

For Edwards, the Lord's Supper was a place of real communion with Christ who was present at the meal. It was a means by which those who were Christ's people might satisfy their spiritual appetites. It was also the place where Christ met, not only with the individual, but with his people and as such there was a communal enjoyment of Christ in a meal that expressed Christian fellowship. Considering what it represented and what it anticipated, Christians in preparation for this meal ought to rid themselves of all rancour. While Edwards may have continued to adhere to the Stoddardean model in practice, his view of what occurred in the Supper indicated that he saw it, not as a converting ordinance, but as a place of true spiritual communion for Christ and his people.

Chapter Four
Self-Examination

The need to prepare for participation in the Lord's Supper, and the need for self-examination as the chief means of preparation, had long been a matter of great importance in the English Reformed tradition. For all writers, the key biblical text in this regard was 1 Corinthians 11:28, 'But let a man examine himself, and so let him eat of that bread, and drink of that cup.' One of the earliest guides to self-examination, *A Treatise of Examination Before and After the Lord's Supper*, came from the pen of Richard Greenham, a contemporary of William Perkins and one of the seminal figures in the development of Puritan theology. Greenham offered the stern warning that 'hee that shall put the things exhibiting the very bodie of Christ into an unprepared heart, and unsanctified soule, shall be most guiltie of that judgement which is pronounced for him, that is, *He is guiltie of the body and blood of Christ.*'[1] In his treatise Greenham set out a number of rules for self examination. The primary rule to be applied was taken from 2 Corinthians 13, '*Prove your selves whether ye are in the faith.* that is, (as I interpret it, and most men of sound iudgement thinke with me,) whether the faith bee in thee, and whether yee have received the spirit of Christ which is his vicar.'[2]

He then offered several other rules for self-examination. A person must judge themselves according to God's law. Having done so 'wee shall finde a great spoyle of obedience in us, and wee shall see our selves marveilously to bee defective.' Then a person must consider how unkindly they have dealt

[1]Greenham, *Workes,* 499.

[2]Greenham, *Workes*, 501.

with the Saviour since their conversion, leading to 'a shame for that which is past, with a greefe for that which is present, and with a feare of that which may come hereafter.'[3] Having subjected themselves to such examination, they would conclude they are an unworthy person and, as such, they would avoid God's condemnation. This sense of unworthiness would lead them to seek the righteousness which Christ alone can provide. In return 'truely God requireth nothing at our hands, but even that small condition Ephes. 4.32. *To be curteous one to another, and tender hearted, forgiving one another even as God for Christs sake for gave vs.*' This was because 'the retaining of enmitie to our brethren doth after a sort more offend God, then our offending against God himselfe.'[4] Greenham stressed two other points. The first was that this was to be self-examination. No-one was to examine another, rather each person must consider their own standing before God. The second point was that 'examination must end in eating and drinking, and not in abstaining.'[5] The purpose of self-examination was not to exclude oneself from the Supper but to prepare oneself to participate in it.

The importance of self-examination continued in the writings of the Puritans with many of their works focusing on the theme of 'worthy receiving.' For example, William Ames set out rules for self-examination so that 'we may with fruit use this Sacrament.' This examination was to be carried out according to the rule of Scripture where 'The dispositions in this trial, principally to be respected, are Faith, Repentance, Charity, and that study of new obedience.'[6] Thomas Watson's first answer to the question of how to prepare for the Lord's Supper was 'We must come with self-examining hearts.'[7] In Matthew Henry's communion handbook he devoted one of the four chapters to the theme of self-examination, noting that in terms of preparation 'the duty most expressly required in our preparation for the ordinance of the Lord's Supper, is that of self-examination.'[8]

The need for self-examination also played a large part in the sacramental culture of New England. Indeed, one of the reasons that Thomas Shepard argued children should not be admitted to the Supper was that they were incapable of self-examination. He explained 'Children not being usually able

[3]Greenham, *Workes,* 501.

[4]Greenham, *Workes*, 502.

[5]Greenham, *Workes,* 502.

[6]Ames, *Conscience,* Book IV, 84, 85.

[7]Watson, *The Holy Eucharist,* 68.

[8]Henry, *Communicant's Companion*, 68.

to examine themselves, nor discern the Lord's body, hence they are not to be admitted to the use of this privilege.'[9] Self-examination was critical to the right reception of the Supper.

In the next generation when Solomon Stoddard advocated changing the rules regarding admission to the Supper, he too had to deal with 1 Corinthians 11:28 and the matter of self-examination. In his 1709 work *An Appeal to the Learned* Stoddard sought to respond to Increase Mather's criticisms of his views. Part of this response included his comments on the Mather's treatment of this verse. He noted that Mather insisted upon two things based on this text with the first being 'that the Examination here required is, whether he has grace in his Soul.'[10] Yet, for Stoddard 'it is most evident, that this is not the Examination that they are stirred up unto.' Rather, it was clear from the context that the examination concerned 'whether they understood the nature of the Ordinance, that so they may solemnly consider what they have to do when they wait upon God in it.'[11] The second thing that Mather insisted upon is 'that the Greek word rendered *Examine,* does import an *Examination to Approbation*.' Stoddard argued that the case was not proven, since the word was used in other senses in the New Testament. In some instances, as with hypocrites, this examination might prove their disapprobation. Even if it meant to examine to approbation, it must be considered whether this meant 'Assurance or a probable hope.' If the former, then none but those who have assurance may attend the Supper. If the latter 'then such persons may come as are not sincere, and then Sanctifying grace is not necessary in order to a lawful attending the Lords-Supper.'[12] For Stoddard, self-examination was not a means to exclude some from the Supper, but an aid to those who would participate in it. In this respect he stood in the mainstream of the English Puritan tradition.

Since Edwards viewed the Lord's Supper as the pre-eminent ordinance and was keen to encourage his congregation to participate in it, he too placed great emphasis upon the need to eat and drink correctly. This meant that before coming to the Supper he saw the necessity of a person examining themselves. Old views Edwards as having an unusual concern with self-examination, stating that when he came to deal with the Supper 'Most of what he has to say concerns the subject of the relationship of the sacrament

[9] Shepard, "Church Membership", 531.

[10] Stoddard, *Appeal to the Learned,* 81.

[11] Stoddard, *Appeal to the Learned,* 82.

[12] Stoddard, *Appeal to the Learned,* 9.

to church discipline.' He adds that he 'seems obsessed with the subject of worthy participation' and that 'all too frequently' his text is 1 Corinthians 11:28.[13] Edwards, however, simply reflected the common concern among Puritans for right participation in the sacrament, and was more hopeful than Old suggests, believing with earlier generations that self-examination, rather than leading to a person's exclusion from the Supper, would help them to participate in it in a more profitable way. This is evident as we turn to his treatment of the key passage of 1 Corinthians 11.

Edwards and 1 Corinthians 11

Contrary to Old's assertion Edwards did not turn 'all too frequently' to 1 Corinthians 11:28. The Edwards Project at Yale records only two sermons on the text, one of which was preached in 1731 and then again in 1756. The other was preached at Stockbridge after his dismissal from Northampton.[14] He also preached four sermons on other related texts from 1 Corinthians 11 where Paul deals with problems at the Lord's Supper in Corinth. We will turn to his treatment of 1 Corinthians 11:28 in his first sermon below, but before that we will consider his notes on this chapter in *The Blank Bible*.

Edwards' notes on the relevant section of 1 Corinthians 11 began with some brief comments on verses 17 and 21. He then wrote more fully on verse 22, 'What? have ye not houses to eat and to drink in? or despise ye the church of God, and shame them that have not? what shall I say to you? shall I praise you in this? I praise you not.' He recorded that Paul was writing in a setting where at the Supper the rich feasted and the poor went away hungry. He remarked that the Supper in the early church was an opportunity for the church not only to share fellowship, but to express charity. In this respect it 'better represented Christ's preparing the gospel feast for the poor, the maimed, the halt, and the blind.' Yet, the situation had arisen in Corinth where the poor 'were denied the spiritual advantage of partaking of the Lord's Supper, for it seems they would not let them partake that could not help bear the charge of the provision.'[15]

He then commented on 1 Corinthians 11:27, 'Wherefore whosoever shall eat this bread, and drink this cup of the Lord, unworthily, shall be guilty of

[13] Old, *Holy Communion*, 606, 607.

[14] See the Sermon Index at http://edwards.yale.edu/research/sermon-index/canonical?chapter=11&book=46. Apart from his sermons Edwards' seldom mentioned the text in his writings and the few significant comments he made were during the Communion Controversy.

[15] *WJE* 24:1050.

the body and blood of the Lord.' Edwards remarked that since the bread and wine were signs of the body and blood of Christ 'those that so contemned, and negligently and profanely treated these signs, they by fair construction slighted the thing signified.' Paul regarded this profanation of the signs so seriously, that he concluded that those who treated it in this manner had 'implicitly manifested a Consent to his death.' In other words, those who profaned the Supper were just as guilty as those who stood by and were accordingly complicit in Christ's crucifixion. A person who ate and drank in this way did so as one who ate and drank the prey they had hunted. They did this 'to satisfy hatred and blood-thirstiness.' This was contrary to those who ate and drank 'from love and gracious appetite' so that they may 'feed on Christ.'[16]

In his treatment of this verse Edwards, perhaps, reflected the sentiments of his favourite Bible commentator Matthew Poole, who wrote that the person who profaned the Supper would be judged 'as if he had crucified Christ, the profanation of Christ's ordinance reflecting upon Christ himself.'[17] In even more emotive language Edwards made the same point in a sermon on Luke 22:48 'You Come to Christ as it were with a Kiss. You Come to meeting & to the sacrament as tho you were friends. Enquire Whether you bent like Judas also in this other Respect that You betray Your Lord.'[18] He also employed this example when commenting on Matthew chapter 26 noting, 'Antichrist is another Judas who, pretending to be the follower of Christ, are his worst enemies in the world, as Judas more incensed God's anger than his crucifiers. So hypocrites in all ages are the betrayers of Christ, who, by a seeming embracing religion, expose Christ to shame and mockery, as Judas with a kiss.'[19] As Stephen Stein comments for Edwards 'Judas had "a kind of faith in Christ," yet he was destitute of true faith and piety.'[20] Such a view of Judas was common among Puritans who considered Judas to be the epitome of one who participated in the Supper and yet did so hypocritically. As Thomas Watson stated, 'Judas sucked Death from the Tree of Life.'[21] Here was the real danger for someone who participated in the Supper in an unworthy manner, that they were guilty of crucifying Christ all

[16] *WJE* 24:1050, 1051.

[17] Poole, *A Commentary,* 581.

[18] No. 128. Luke 22:48, *WJEO* 44.

[19] *WJE* 15:54.

[20] *WJE* 24:938, footnote 6.

[21] Watson, *The Holy Eucharist,* 21.

over again or behaving like Judas who sat with Christ at the table and yet betrayed him.

In dealing with 1 Corinthians 11 Edwards reserved his longest note for verse 28 'But let a man examine himself, and so let him eat of that bread, and drink of that cup.' In considering this statement he focused on the Greek phrase καὶ οὕτως. He noted that these words are rightly translated 'and so' but that such a translation might be misleading for the English reader. He pointed out that a person might infer no more from these words than a sequence of events, where a person examined himself and then ate. Edwards, however, followed the translation of John Locke, stating 'the Apostle implies no more than this, that they should with great care and strictness see to it that they conformed their eating the Lord's Supper to the institution which the Apostle had now particularly laid before them.' He said this was clear from the context where the Corinthians were not acting properly in their celebration of the Supper. Examining oneself meant taking 'notice of the use and end of the bread and wine.'[22]

When he turned to verse 29, he noted that eating and drinking unworthily, and without self-examination, would lead to a person being exposed to 'God's condemnation and judgement.' Once more, however, his focus was not only upon the theme of condemnation but also upon the purpose of the Supper, that we might have 'have justification and life.' This was the benefit for those who ate and drank worthily. For those who did so unworthily it would 'avail 'em nothing to their justification and salvation, but on the contrary will be to their condemnation.'[23] This was a common view amongst Puritans with William Perkins remarking 'If you come not furnished on this manner to the Lord's Table, you shall be adjudged guilty of the body and blood of Christ, as he is guilty of high treason who does counterfeit or clip the prince's coin.'[24]

In his final remarks on this chapter Edwards dealt with vs31,32. Here he noted the importance of personal judgement or self-examination. He concluded that 'If we would examine and judge ourselves, we should not be judged; or if we were judged, it would not be to condemnation, but only as being chastened as children, that we might escape condemnation.' The

[22] *WJE* 24:1051.

[23] *WJE* 24:1051, 1052.

[24] Perkins, *The Golden Chain*, 169.

means of doing this is to 'critically try our behavior by the institutions and rules of Christ, taking care strictly to conform ourselves thereto.'[25]

Edwards notes on 1 Corinthians 11 reflect the Apostle Paul's emphasis on the need for self-examination, but like the apostle this was not a call to be excessively introspective. Rather, his comments are balanced by the need to grasp the positive meaning of the Supper. Furthermore, as his remarks on vs31,32 make clear the aim of self-examination was not to discourage participation, but to persuade participants to be rightly prepared to take this meal and benefit from it. As noted above, this was a longstanding theme among Puritan writers, that the purpose of examination was not exclusion but right participation.

Edwards struck a similar note in his first sermon on 1 Corinthians 10:16, referred to in the previous chapter. Here he exhorted his congregation 'Before we Come to [the ordinance] Let us Carefully & strictly examine our selves.' He then set out, in typical fashion, a list of criteria by which this self-examination might be conducted. Congregants might consider,

> whether we [live] in any way [of] sin. [W]hether we neglect any duty that God hath Required of us. [W]hether or no we bent too Careless in the Performance of some duties. [W]hether we bent Got in a negligent way of Performing duties of Religion. [W]hether or no we bent too little watch full [of] our own hearts & don't too Easily Give way to temptations to neglect our duty. [W]hether we bent too little in Reading the word of G[od]. [W]hether we bent too flightly & overtly in Prayer. We must examine our selves whether or no we don't live in some way of Commission that is Provoking unto God or at Least often fall into some sin for want of our Resolving & watching against [it]. [W]hether or no we don't harbour & Indulge some lust or other.

Having undergone such self-examination, he added 'Let us therefore take heed to ourselves at all times before we Come to the Lord's Supper to search & try ourselves & see if there be any wicked way in us. Let us think on our ways & turn our feet into Gods testimonies. Humbling our selves for our Past sins & taking serious Resolutions of future amendment.'[26] Again, it is clear that the goal of self-examination was not exclusion but suitable self-preparation. It is also evident that, only a person who had

[25] *WJE* 24:1052.

[26] No. 156. 1 Corinthians 10:16(a), *WJEO* 45.

already experienced the work of regeneration, and who could undertake such an examination, could hope to benefit from the Supper.

Self-Examination and 1 Corinthians 11

Edwards' most extensive treatment of 1 Corinthians 11 and the need for self-examination is found in a sermon on vs 28,29 preached in 1731. As Mark Valeri has pointed out, the issues addressed in this sermon were ones which greatly occupied his mind as this time. This is reflected in several entries in the *Miscellanies* which date from the same period.[27] What becomes clear from the sermon is that Edwards' reflections on the Supper are not easily tied down to a single trope as he sought to apply the message of this passage to the varied conditions of his congregants.

Edwards opened the sermon by explaining the problem in Corinth where there was disorder in their assemblies and in particular 'unworthy attendance on the Lord's Supper.'[28] This was caused by the fact that the Corinthians had lost sight of the purpose of the Supper and were using it simply as an occasion for eating and drinking. This profane use, as he called it, may have been caused by familiarity due to the frequency of its celebration in the early church. The Corinthians added to this profanation by making their celebration an occasion for gluttony and drunkenness. This led the apostle, not only to rebuke them, but to remind them of the true nature of the Supper. Echoing his comments in *The Blank Bible,* he pointed out that the Corinthians' lack of solemnity at the Supper 'showed an unaffectedness at his death itself, and thereby a kind of consent to the act of the murderers.'[29] The scene in Corinth was a reminder of the dangers of eating and drinking unworthily at the Lord's Supper and led Edwards to state his doctrine that 'Persons ought to examine themselves of their fitness before they presume to partake of the Lord's Supper, lest by their unworthy partaking, they eat and drink damnation to themselves.'[30]

As the sermon unfolded, he turned his attention to the question of what it meant for a person to be fit, or unfit, to participate in the Supper. As he did so his first thought was for those with tender consciences. Speaking about fitness to celebrate the Supper he commented there is no-one on earth

[27] Editor's Introduction, *WJE* 17:263.

[28] *WJE* 17:264.

[29] *WJE* 17:266.

[30] *WJE* 17:266.

who is in the right condition to do so since just as 'we are unworthy of these gospel blessings themselves, so we are unworthy of the means, the signs, and the offers of them.'[31] He added, however, that it is 'not every unfitness that renders the attendance defective and sinful in that manner.' For the reality was that a person had 'so much sin in his heart that he can no other than attend the Lord's Supper in a very defective manner.' Indeed, this same sinfulness 'renders [us] unfit to pray to God or come into his presence in any duty of worship.'[32] Sinfulness should not preclude a person from performing their religious duties. While the Supper might be important as a means of grace, it should not be avoided out of a sense of unworthiness. Rather, that sense of unworthiness should draw a person to the sacrament in the same sense that it draws them to prayer and preaching.

The idea that a person should not neglect the ordinances, including the Supper, had a long pedigree in the Puritan tradition. Matthew Henry had argued that 'You dare not come to this sacrament; yet you dare pray, you dare hear the Word. I know you dare not neglect either the one or the other; and what is the sacrament but doing the same thing by "a visible sign," which is and ought to be done in effect by the Word and prayer?'[33] Solomon Stoddard used a modified version of this argument by stating that a person should attend the Supper just as they attended the other ordinances. In response to the objection that it was mockery for an unregenerate person to attend the Lord's Table he argued, 'It is no more a mocking of God than for such Persons to pray; by this argument they may not Pray.'[34] It reflected his view that the Supper should not be set above the other ordinances.

Although not every sin excluded a person nonetheless, according to Edwards, there was a particular kind of unfitness for the sacrament that 'renders the ordinance void.' For, while a person 'may be qualified so as to have a right to come by the gospel,' they may 'attend the ordinance in a very defective manner.'[35] It was this particular kind of unfitness that ought to cause a person to examine themselves. As he continued to explain there were four specific ways in which self-examination ought to occur, so that a person might attend the Supper in a fitting manner.

[31] *WJE* 17:266.

[32] *WJE* 17:267.

[33] Henry, *Communicant's Companion,* 58.

[34] Stoddard, *Appeal to the Learned,* 46.

[35] *WJE* 17:267.

In the first instance a person ought to examine themselves regarding whether they were living in some known sin. A person who lived an immoral life was unworthy to come to the table. Their sin might be one of omission or commission; it might be great, or it might be small. Just as under the old covenant a person was excluded from the Passover and eating the sacrifices because they were unclean, so those who 'live in the customary indulgence of any lust whatsoever, they are utterly unfit to come to the holy ordinance of the Lord.'[36] In his sermon on 1 Corinthians 5:7, Edwards pointed to the Passover as a type of the Supper, stating 'The sacrament of the Lord's Sup[per] is the memorial of the sacrif[ice] of Christ our Passover that is sacrificed for us. The sacrament of the L[ord's] Supp[er] succeeds in the Room of the Pas[sover] & may be Called the [Chris]tian Passover.'[37] In the crucifixion '[Christ] was offered in sac[rifice] to G[od]. The Paschal Lamb was slain as a sacrif[ice] to G[od] to atone for their sins. But herein it was but a type of [Christ] who is the only True sacrif[ice] who is the Great sa[vior] & only Propitiating sac[rifice] of which all the Legal sacrif[ices] were but shad[ows].' As a consequence, since Christ was the reality to whom the Passover pointed, the demands for those participating in the new covenant meal could not be less stringent than those for taking part in the old one.

The second area in which a person ought to examine themselves was in consideration of whether they had a 'serious resolution to avoid all sin and live in obedience to all known commands as long as he lives.'[38] If they participated in the Supper with the design of sinning afterwards or were poised to commit sin as the occasion arose, then they were not fit to attend the sacrament. His suggestion that this was a matter for self-examination demonstrates that he was not content with the outward conformity of living a scandal free life that Stoddard had accepted. For Edwards, a person must look deeper and examine their inner motivation. It was a theme that he returned to in a much more direct manner in a sermon he preached on Romans 3:19. Speaking on the text 'That every mouth may be stopped' he addressed the congregation in forthright terms,

> How have some of you attended that sacred ordinance of the Lord's Supper, without any manner of serious preparation, and

[36] *WJE* 17:267.

[37] No. 294. 1 Corinthians 5:7, *WJEO* 48.

[38] *WJE* 17:268.

> in a careless slighty frame of spirit, and chiefly to comply with custom! Have you not ventured to put the sacred symbols of the body and blood of Christ into your mouth, while at the same time you lived in ways of known sins and intended no other than still to go on in the same wicked practices? And it may be have sat at the Lord's table, with rancor in your heart against some of your brethren, that you have sat there with. You have come even to that holy feast of love among God's children, with the leaven of malice and envy in your heart; and so have eat and drank judgment to yourself.[39]

The sermon echoed his words on 1 Corinthians 5:7 where he warned that in taking the Supper 'we ought to Keep it without spiritual Leaven' just as the Israelites were to keep the Passover by removing actual leaven.[40] The person who attended the sacrament in an unworthy manner, brought judgement upon themselves. Notably, Edwards numbered those who attended the sacrament merely out of custom as being among those who were unworthy participants.

The third area in which he urged examination developed this argument further as he noted that a person should consider if they 'entertain a spirit of hatred or envy or revenge towards their neighbor.'[41] If a person did not set aside such an attitude, then 'he eats and drinks unworthily' for such a spirit 'renders a man unfit and makes the ordinance void.'[42] Once more he made a comparison with the Passover equating this spirit of revenge with leaven in the house. He spoke of the need not only to exercise self-examination, but also to practice forgiveness and to put an end to any quarrel. In his sermon on 1 Corinthians 5:7 he made the same point that if 'the Chil[dren] of Is[rael] Could not Expect that the Pass[over] would be blessed if they Kept it with Leaven Can a Church that tolerates scandal at the Table of the L[ord]? One scandalous Person so tolerated Pollutes the whole Church.'[43] For Edwards recognising the importance of the corporate dimensions of the Supper was vital for its proper celebration.

[39] *WJE* 19:351.

[40] No. 294. 1 Corinthians 5:7, *WJEO* 48.

[41] *WJE* 17:268.

[42] *WJE* 17:269.

[43] No. 294. 1 Corinthians 5:7, *WJEO* 48.

Finally, he pointed out that a person ought to exercise self-examination in terms of their purpose in coming to the Supper. They should consider if they were coming to the Supper bearing in mind the 'ends for which the ordinance was appointed.' He said that they may come 'only for some end, some temporal advantage or credit', in particular coming 'merely that their children mayn't lie under the disgrace of being unbaptized.'[44] Here he had in view those who saw full church membership as a means to obtain the baptism of their children, and, for whom, the Supper was a mere formality that was far removed from its true purpose. In this way they were guilty of the Corinthian error of eating and drinking without discerning the Lord's body.

This theme of taking the Supper only to ensure that children would be baptized was one that Edwards came back to in the Communion Controversy in the 1740s. In his *Humble Inquiry* he remarked that with regard to owning the covenant and coming to the Supper it was 'visibly a prevailing custom for persons to neglect this, till they come to be married, and then to do it for their credit's sake, and that their children may be baptized.'[45] Indeed, in a letter to Rev. Thomas Foxcroft at the height of the controversy, he wrote that while his people might in time be won over to his views on the Lord' Supper 'the greatest difficulty of all relating to my principles is here, respecting baptism' of which there was 'scarce hope' of reconciling them.[46]

After considering the four areas in which self-examination ought to occur Edwards turned his attention to why this preparation was vital. While those who ate and drank worthily had the promise of salvation sealed to them, those who did so unworthily 'seal their own damnation.'[47] He offered two reasons why this was the case. The first was that the person who participated in the Supper while continuing in their sin showed 'horrid contempt of the ordinance and the things signified in it.'[48] Reflecting his remarks in *The Blank Bible,* he said that such a person participated in the murder of Christ and fed upon him 'as a wild beast eats his prey.' In doing so 'They eat and drink their own damnation because they therein expressed such a contempt of that which is their only remedy from damnation, viz. the body and blood

[44] *WJE* 17:269

[45] *WJE* 12:213.

[46] *WJE* 16:283.

[47] *WJE* 17:270.

[48] *WJE* 17:270.

of Jesus Christ.'[49] The second reason they sealed their own damnation was by their dissimulation and consequent mockery of the sacrament. The Supper was a covenant meal in which Christ sealed the covenant with his people and they sealed themselves to him. Yet, if a person at the Supper sealed themselves 'while never so much as seriously to purpose any such thing and, much more, when they actually at the same time do live allowedly in things directly contrary' then it was a horrible piece of mockery. It was mere pretence that they were giving themselves to Christ while they planned to rise from the table and return once more to their sinful course of action.[50]

Edwards concluded the sermon with a brief and pointed application. It was a warning to 'all persons carefully to examine themselves before they come to the Lord's Supper, that they don't seal their own damnation.' He noted, however, that such self-examination and being found wanting did not mean exclusion from the Supper. Rather, 'the end of examination is that you may amend before you come.' Again, it is evident that his goal was to encourage participation, even if he ended on the sombre note 'If you live in any known way of wickedness, don't come here to eat and drink damnation to yourselves.'[51]

As noted in chapter 2 Edwards preached a sermon on 1 Corinthians 11:29 in 1733.[52] In this sermon his doctrine was 'The sacrament of the Lord's Supper is a very sacred Ordinance.' When he turned to the application of the sermon his first thought was for those who were invited to the Lord's Supper but refused to come. He pointed out that 'we are Invited to Come freely. No hard terms are Exacted of us but we are Invited to Come without money & without Price.' This led him to conclude 'Therefore Persons Going away... must necessarily be a visible dishonour & Contempt of this.' He said that for such a show of contempt people would be answerable to God.

He then discussed the reasons why a person might neglect the Supper. Here he dealt with the common excuse that people felt they were unworthy to come to the Sacrament. He argued that such a person may in fact be exhibiting a lack of desire to come and participate in God's appointed means of salvation. This reluctance was rooted in their unwillingness 'to forsake all sin for the sake of it & seek it in all the ways of Gods appointment.' In particular, he made the distinction between being unworthy and unfit,

[49]*WJE* 17:271.

[50]*WJE* 17:271.

[51]*WJE* 17:272.

[52]No. 270. 1 Corinthians 11:29, *WJEO* 48.

noting that the person who is truly aware of their unworthiness is in fact 'Evangelically fit.' What rendered a person unfit was their unwillingness to part with their sinful ways. Such a person was all 'the more Exceedingly Guilty & inexcusable' because it showed that the way in which they live 'is a way of Known wicked[ness].' The person who truly understood their corruption would see 'so much the more need to Go. Come & Receive Christ's body & blood.' Even the person who knew that their sinfulness rendered them unfit to attend the Supper should see that this meant they must seek God and the salvation that he offered. The sermon only briefly mentioned the need for self-examination in preparation for coming to the Supper.

Once again it is clear that Edwards' primary aim was to encourage participation in the Supper, not to chasten his congregants or put obstacles in their way. As David Hall comments on this sermon 'The theme was the familiar one of urging people to hasten to the Lord's Table and not worry overmuch about the injunction to examine themselves.'[53] The themes taken up by Edwards in this sermon were ones that he returned to again. His magnanimity in terms of people coming to the Supper as a means of grace is captured in a letter written to Rev. Elnathan Whitman of Hartford, Connecticut in 1743/4. Here, reflecting on the Apostle Paul's response to the disorder in the Corinthian church, he wrote,

> the Apostle never so much as gave any direction for the suspension of any one member from the Lord's Supper on account of these disorders or from any other part of the public worship of God; but instead of that, gives 'em directions how they shall go on better to attend the Lord's Supper and other parts of worship. And he himself, without suspension or interruption, goes On to call and treat them as beloved brethren, Christians, sanctified in Christ Jesus, called to be saints, and praises God on their behalf for the grace that is given them by Christ Jesus; and often and abundantly expresses his charity towards them in innumerable expressions that I might mention. And nothing is more apparent than that he don't treat them as those with respect to whom there lies a bar in the way of others' treating them with the charity that belongs to saints and good and honest members of the Christian church, till the bar be removed by a church process.[54]

[53]Editor's Introduction, *WJE* 12: 44.

[54]*WJE* 16:131.

Demonstrating his positive view of the Supper Edwards later pointed out in *Misrepresentations Corrected* that he had 'been immediately concerned in the admission of more than three quarters of the Northampton's present members.'[55] His emphasis on self-examination was not to exclude members of his congregation, but to treat them charitably and have them participate in the Supper in a spiritually profitable manner. The greatest need, in terms of self-examination, was to avoid self-deception about one's true standing with God, and to then turn to God and participate in the Supper in a beneficial way.

Self-Examination and Self-Deceit

The theme of hypocrisy was an important one in Puritan writings, both in England and New England. For Edwards it was a matter of deep concern throughout his life. The dangers of hypocrisy were all too evident to him in a church-going culture where there was always the danger of practicing a form of Christianity that did little more than satisfy social norms. While his anxieties about hypocrisy intensified in the aftermath of the Great Awakening, and were expressed most fully in *Religious Affections*, it is a theme found in his work from earliest times. William Stoever notes, that as early as the 1720s Edwards began 'to specify the content and character of true godliness.'[56] It was in many respects an interest that arose from his own early and protracted spiritual experience. As he reflected on this in his *Personal Narrative*, written around 1740, he concluded 'many are deceived with such affections, and such a kind of delight, as I then had in religion, and mistake it for grace.'[57] The heart of Edwards' anxiety was, ultimately, a pastoral one. The real danger for hypocrites was not that they might deceive others by their pretence, but that they might deceive themselves and, consequently, fall under the wrath of God. As Ava Chamberlain has written 'Modern-day hypocrites wilfully deceive by constructing a false façade of virtue or piety... Edwards thought hypocrisy primarily signifies not the self-conscious and willful intention to deceive others. The deception of others is included in the meaning of the term but is a secondary by-product of

[55] *WJE* 12:358, 359.

[56] Stoever, "The Godly Will's Discerning", 91.

[57] *WJE* 16:791. For a discussion of Edwards' on true and false conversion see Luke, "The 'reception of Christ", 321–334.

hypocrites own self-deception.'[58] It was this same concern for those who were self-deceived that led Edwards to encourage self-examination before the Supper where a person eating and drinking in an unworthy manner was in danger of bringing damnation upon themselves. As Chamberlain says, in such a case their 'very hope for salvation rested upon a tragically uncertain foundation.'[59]

In a sermon preached in 1728/29 based on the parable of the sower, Edwards took as his text Matthew 13:23, 'But he that received seed into the good ground is he that heareth the word, and understandeth it; which also beareth fruit, some an hundredfold, some sixty, some thirty.' In the sermon he developed three doctrines, all focused on the need for Christians to bear fruit. He observed that 'hypocrites are the same in profession as the godly: they come to meeting as God's people, and it may be come to the sacrament as God's people; they go along with the godly and make in many things as fair a show as they: but their fruits are not the same. When ye come there, they are as different as wheat and tares.'[60] Across all his writings bearing fruit was, for Edwards, the great mark of authentic Christianity which distinguished the genuine professor from the hypocrite. As he wrote in *Religious Affections*, his fullest treatise on the signs of true and false religion 'Christian practice or a holy life is a great and distinguishing sign of true and saving grace.'[61] In this sermon he remarked that true 'Spiritual understanding is not mere speculation that rests in the head and reaches not the heart. It is not of an unactive or barren nature, but will surely be producing of good fruits.'[62] Accordingly, this meant that a person must examine themselves to see if there was evidence of such fruit, and 'this must be done especially before a sacrament: there should be a set and solemn examination of this nature at such a time, according to that rule, 1 Corinthians 11:28, "Let a man examine himself, and so let him eat." This he must do lest he eat and drink judgment to himself.'[63] Such examination was not, however, to be conducted in a perfunctory manner in the period immediately before the Supper. Rather, 'There must be a continual watching over your own heart every now and then, examining and searching to see if

[58] Chamberlain, "Hypocrisy and the Religious Life", 338.

[59] Chamberlain, "Hypocrisy and the Religious Life", 339.

[60] *WJE* 14:256, 257.

[61] *WJE* 2:406.

[62] *WJE* 14:256.

[63] *WJE* 14: 276.

you can't find some wicked way in you. Try your heart: see if you can't find some instances wherein it is unchristian and contrary to the rule of God's Word.'[64] The antidote to hypocrisy was continual watchfulness.

This theme of the danger of engaging in hypocrisy when coming to the Lord's Supper was more fully developed in a sermon preached in 1731/32 on Ezekiel 23:37–39 where he dealt with the subject of spiritual adultery. Considering vs 37 'That they have committed adultery, and blood is in their hands, and with their idols have they committed adultery, and have also caused their sons, whom they bare unto me, to pass for them through the fire, to devour them' he noted Israel's dual sins of idolatry and the accompanying infanticide. Building on this his doctrine was 'When They that attend Ordinances in violations of Plain & Known Commands of God they are Guilty of Profaning these ordinances.'[65] He then noted, by way of explanation, that an ordinance in its broadest sense could be any divine institution or appointment. By this definition marriage, for example, was an ordinance. More particularly, however, the means of worship were ordinances, and he wanted to warn his listeners against profaning such ordinances.

He explained how the ordinances of worship such as prayer, praise, preaching, and church discipline were all sanctified by God for the use of his people. Such ordinances were then dreadfully profaned by those who attended them while living wicked lives yet, pretending they were using them as a means of approaching God. In doing so, they showed irreverence and contempt for God and mocked him. Given the high regard in which Edwards held the Supper as the place where Christ particularly meets with his people, profaning this sacrament was especially heinous. So, he spoke of those who came to the Supper pretending,

> that they desired to be fed with spiritual Nourishment & to be Conformed & assimilated to Christ & have Communion with him but they declare by their [actions] that they have no Regard to Christ & that they had Rather have their Lusts Gratified than to be fed with his spiritual food. They show that they don't desire any assimilation to Christ but to be different from him & opposite.

When it came to the application of the sermon he focused on the need for self-examination. He especially warned against the danger of 'pretending', a

[64] *WJE* 14:276.

[65] No. 222. Ezekiel 23:37–39, *WJEO* 46.

term he used over twenty times. Self-examination must be exercised above all when coming to the Supper which is,

> that holy & sacred ordinance Instituted for the special Commemoration of the Greatest & most wonderfull of all divine acts towards mankind & for the special & visible Representation of the most Glorious & wonderfull things of our Religion & for the most solemn Profession & Renewal of the Covenant of Grace & our Engagements to God & for that more special Communion with Jesus Christ.

He continued to consider how it was necessary to have scrupulous examination in such areas as dealings with others, behaviour in the home and towards neighbours, various lusts, excessive eating and drinking, vain conversation and Sabbath breaking.

He then added a further word of caution that 'Persons are very Ready to deal Exceeding Treacherous in the matter of self Examination.' The danger was not that people may be too thorough in their examination, rather they were 'exceeding Partial to themselves. They spare themselves.' As such, their examination was not according to truth, as they were blind and persuaded and flattered themselves about their true condition, even in the face of known sin. People could excuse themselves from even the most flagrant sins in their lives. Consequently, he pointed out, 'Persons Commonly live wickedly & Go to hell in those ways that they flatter themselves are Lawfull.' They must, however, think carefully about the dangers of such self-deception because God was never more provoked than he was by those who covered up their sin and then profaned the ordinances by their participation. Such behaviour broke the third commandment which prohibited taking God's name in vain. Edwards marvelled aloud that God did not consume such people on the spot, declaring 'Tis a wonder of God's Patience that he don't break forth upon you [and] strike you dead in a moment for You Profane holy things in a far more dreadfull manner than Uzza did whom yet God struck dead for his sin[ful] Errour. & whereas he was struck dead for one Profanation you do it from week to week & from day to day.'

His warnings in this sermon were strict and vivid. They were also very necessary given the dangers that awaited those who profaned that which God had declared holy. He urged his congregation to stringent, soul-searching examination because of the dangers of settling on an outward profession of religion. As Paul Ramsey has written for Edwards since 'all visible signs may be common to both converted and unconverted men. . . judging other men by outward appearances is at best uncertain.'[66] It was necessary, therefore, for self-examination to go beyond the superficial in search of the signs of true godliness. As his ministry progressed the signs of true and false religion was a theme that Edwards returned to repeatedly. It was his concern about this that led him in the aftermath of the revival and Northampton's return to its former ways to urge the church to renew the covenant in 1742. Part of that renewal was a promise stating,

> And being sensible of our own weakness, and the deceitfulness of our own hearts, and our proneness to forget our most solemn vows and lose our resolutions; we promise to be often strictly examining ourselves by these promises, especially before the sacrament of the Lord's Supper; and beg of God that he would, for Christ's sake keep us from wickedly dissembling in these our solemn vows; and that he who searches our hearts [Romans 8:27] and ponders the path of our feet [Proverbs 4:26] would from time to time help us in trying ourselves by this covenant, and help us to keep covenant with him and not leave us to our own foolish, wicked and treacherous hearts.[67]

Self-examination before the Supper was vital given the frailties and deceitfulness of the human heart. From this quotation we see that the examination that was required was not something that was merely routine, but it was an exercise requiring divine assistance. No-one could truly know their own heart apart from God's help. With this in mind, it is difficult to imagine that Edwards was calling those who knew nothing of the Spirit's work in their lives to examine themselves and then sit at the table in the hope that the Supper might then act as a means to conversion. It appears more likely that he believed that such people would eat and drink damnation to themselves.

The Lord's Supper and the Gospel

John Gerstner argues that Edwards saw the Lord's Supper as one of the 'propitious times' to seek God. He says that initially he 'tacitly agreed with Solomon Stoddard's doctrine of the Eucharist as a "converting ordinance."' He continues that 'the duty of using the Sacrament in seeking salvation is

[66]Editor's Introduction, *WJE* 2:60.

[67]*WJE* 16:124, 125.

made very clear' in his sermon on Proverbs 8:34. He draws attention to Edwards' statement that it 'ought to be diligently & Carefully attended by all that set themselves to seek the Grace of God.'[68] He also points to his words in a sermon on Isaiah 40:29–31 where he urged his listeners to 'the use of the means of his appointment in attending his ordinances.' Gerstner comments 'We suppose that "ordinances" include sacraments.'[69]

Despite proffering these examples, Gerstner may read too much into them. In his Proverbs sermon Edwards reminded his readers that God's grace was to be sought as they waited upon him and used his appointed means, including natural and revealed religion, moral duties and, especially, observing the Sabbath, and attending preaching and the sacrament.[70] It appears, however, that these instructions were directed primarily to the converted, rather than the unconverted. He noted in the sermon that 'Grace is but Christ dwelling in the soul by his spirit.' When he urged his congregation to use the appointed means he was encouraging them to live in accordance with the indwelling Spirit, not to seek salvation for the first time. This is apparent, for example, in his instructions with respect to moral living. For Edwards, a person could not live a moral life without having first received the Holy Spirit. Furthermore, he warned against the dangers of 'depending on our own Endeavours in the Use of means' and using the means 'to Reform their lives & do moral & Religious duties.' In his view performing religious duties did not draw an unconverted person closer to God. As he stated in the sermon on Isaiah 40:29–31, there was a danger that a person 'Can attend all ordinances' while 'the Heart with Respect to 'em is treacherous.' In such a case they were putting their trust not in the power of God but in things that lie 'within the Reach of man's natural ability with Common assistance.'[71]

It is difficult to make the case from Edwards' writings, even the early ones, that he was ever convinced that the Supper was a converting ordinance. He believed, nonetheless, that conversion might be the incidental fruit of preparing for its celebration. In exhorting people to prepare for the Supper he also had an opportunity to call upon his unconverted hearers to 'seek

[68] Gerstner, *Edwards Evangelist*, 106, 107.

[69] Gerstner, *Edwards Evangelist*, 107, 108.

[70] No. 208. Proverbs 8:34, *WJEO* 46.

[71] No. 597. Isaiah 40:29–31(a), *WJEO* 57.

God & your salvation.'[72] He was clear that for a person to truly benefit from the Supper they must first accept the gospel which it displayed.

In his 1741 sacrament sermon on Psalm 72:6 we see another example of how Edwards used the occasion to preach the gospel to the unconverted. In preaching the Psalm, he treated it in typological fashion, viewing Christ as the rain which comes down as he communicates his benefits. The subjects of those benefits are those who have been mown down. This led him to his doctrine 'Christ, in communicating himself and dispensing his benefits, does as it were come down as the rain on the mown grass.'[73]

He noted that Christ may be said to come down in several senses. He came down in his Incarnation, he will come down in judgement, he comes down in acts of providence and he 'comes down from heaven in the saving influences of his Spirit on the hearts of men... Thus when a sinner is converted, Christ does as it were come down from heaven and enter into the heart to dwell there.'[74] He then explained that there were also several ways in which people may be said to be mown down like grass. In the first instance, all are mown down in the Fall. He explained that 'Man in his first state was as grass that flourishes and grows up. He was in great prosperity... But Satan found means to cut him down.'[75] Then at times the church is said to be cut down 'by general corruption or persecution.'[76] Furthermore, people may be cut down by personal affliction and they may be cut down as an essential part of their humiliation and mortification since 'that which naturally flourishes in the heart of men, it must be mown down.'[77] Also, death may be said to be a way in which people are cut down. Cutting down was essential since 'He must be cut off as to that life that he lives by nature in order to the renewed life by Christ.'[78] It is to such people that Christ comes down 'like the rain on the mown grass... descending upon them he refreshes, revives and restores them as the rain doth the grass after it is mown.'[79]

[72]No. 270. 1 Corinthians 11:29, *WJEO* 48.

[73]*WJE* 22:301.

[74]*WJE* 22:303.

[75]*WJE* 22:304.

[76]*WJE* 22:306.

[77]*WJE* 22:306.

[78]*WJE* 22:307.

[79]*WJE* 22:308.

Edwards reassured his hearers that although through the Fall 'they have utterly ruined themselves, though they are dead in sin naturally, and that death be never so much confirmed by actual sin and a contracted hardness of heart' yet Christ was able to give them life and restore them. He told them 'Though God's favor be utterly lost, though God has been so much provoked and never so dreadful a damnation deserved, yet there is enough in Christ to restore to the favor of God, and to bring into the state of his children and to make happy in God's everlasting smiles.' He continued,

> There is enough in Christ to restore rest, peace and comfort to those who are as it were cut down to the earth with terror of conscience, whose burden and distress has been so great as quite to sink the soul. And though its hope has been as it were cut off and all comfort seemed to be gone, and the soul was brought to give up itself as lost, yet there is enough in Christ to heal souls under such wounds, to raise up out of the dust with the most excellent refreshment, to give light in the greatest darkness. He can raise up as it were out of the depths of hell; he can take out of the miry clay and most horrible pit and set the foot upon a rock.[80]

He remarked that Christ was able to give life to the dead and restore the image of God in fallen humanity. He added that when Christ comes down, he 'restores those souls that have been as it were cut down by the scythe of the law.'[81] In Puritan thought such legal conviction was the necessary prelude to faith and repentance.

When Edwards turned to the application he called first for self-examination. He asked his listeners to examine themselves as to whether they have ever been mown down regarding their own sense of self-sufficiency. More importantly, he asked them if they had ever been cut down by 'a gracious work of God upon your heart, making you poor in spirit.' In other words, this was not merely a legal self-examination since 'legal humiliation is all a mere farce.' Rather, they should examine themselves to see if they recognised a change of disposition that resulted in a 'desire with all your heart that Christ and his worthiness and his righteousness alone should be made mention of.'[82] His application then turned to the second focus of the text, that his hearers

[80] *WJE* 22:309.

[81] *WJE* 22:311.

[82] *WJE* 22:313.

should examine themselves regarding whether they have 'ever have experienced the refreshing, reviving influences of the Spirit of Christ upon your hearts, as of the rain on the mown grass.'[83] Notably, it was only those who had experienced this reviving by Christ who could then seal the covenant once again at the Lord's Table.[84] This foreshadowed his argument made several years later during the Communion Controversy that 'it is evident that every adult person that comes to those seals of the covenant of grace must by his own act own the covenant of grace, and by his own actual profession enter into covenant with God by that covenant. But no man could do this without professing saving faith, for 'tis that, and that only, is the condition of the covenant of grace.'[85]

Finally, Edwards turned his attention to an exhortation addressed to those who had not yet found salvation. He called on them to seek to be like mown grass and have their sense of worthiness and righteousness cut down. They must also be mown down 'by an entirely final renouncing all the objects of your lusts, whatever lusts they be.' It is to those who would be thus mown down that Edwards offered the message of the gospel. He issued an invitation stating, 'Let me from this doctrine take occasion to invite those whose souls are wounded with a sense of their sins and miserable state to come to Christ.' He also presented them with the remedy of one who 'will heal your wounds, will sweetly revive your hearts, renew, strengthen.'[86]

After his dismissal from Northampton there is another example of how Edwards used a sacramental sermon as an occasion to preach the gospel. He took as his text Psalm 1:3 'He shall be like a tree planted by the rivers of water.' The sermon is a simple, extended meditation on this phrase as he prepared the Mahican Indians for the Supper. He stated his doctrine as 'Christ is to the heart of a true saint like a river to the roots of a tree that is planted by it.' Having briefly examined the text he closed the sermon with two applications. In the first he called on his congregation to 'Examine whether you are a true saint. Has your soul been ever like a tree planted by this river?' This was followed by an exhortation to sinners 'to seek an interest in Jesus Christ. If you are not in Christ, though you may be like green trees, yet by and by you will wither. All your streams will fail you.'[87] Preparation

[83] *WJE* 22:315.

[84] *WJE* 22:316.

[85] *WJE* 25:362.

[86] *WJE* 22:318.

[87] *WJE* 25:604.

for the Supper was an occasion to declare the gospel to the unconverted, rather than expecting them to be converted by coming to the Sacrament. While Edwards was now free from the expectations of Northampton his model had not changed. It was in preparation that the gospel was preached, and that sinners might come to repentance. It was not the Supper itself that was the instrument of conversion.

Old's representation of Edwards as someone obsessed with qualification and self-examination requires a degree of correction. Edwards was concerned about the right administration of the Supper, and about the importance of it being received by those who were properly qualified. He also stressed the importance of self-examination. In doing this he was not unusual but was in step with both his predecessors and contemporaries in the Puritan tradition. Even his grandfather agreed that such matters were of the utmost importance. While Edwards stressed the right administration of the Supper and correct participation in it, he nonetheless held a generous spirit by which he sought to encourage congregants to come to the sacrament, which he saw as a duty, and in doing so he exhorted them to do this in a way that would be spiritually profitable. While the idea of the Supper as a converting ordinance did not sit comfortably with him in terms of its essential purpose, he was quite prepared to use its celebration as an occasion to preach the gospel to those who sat in the congregation and who adopted the outward formalities of religion without ever having experienced a true work of regeneration.

Chapter Five
Admission to the Supper

Differences regarding the terms of admission to the Lord's Supper were part of the theological heritage that Edwards had to manage when he came to Northampton. On the one hand he had grown up under the influence of his father Timothy who was prepared to baptize the children of baptized but unconverted parents, receiving them as members of the covenant but he required 'a "relation of experience" and evidence of conversion for admission to full membership and the Lord's Supper.' On the other hand, in Northampton his grandfather, Solomon Stoddard, 'admitted all such baptized children of the covenant to the Supper'[1] which was now the received practice in the church. For much of the course of his ministry in Northampton Edwards accepted his grandfather's inheritance before turning his back upon it in, what seemed to many, to be a sudden conversion to views more like those of his father. As the previous chapters have sought to demonstrate, there was always a degree of tension in his thinking about the Supper and while, at the time, he appeared to change his mind somewhat unexpectedly, this was in reality the public manifestation of long-term misgivings about the practice in Northampton. It was also the natural extension of his understanding of what occurred during the celebration of the Supper. This chapter will focus on Edwards' views on admission, how he dealt with the matter privately in the *Miscellanies* and how he then defended his views as the Communion Controversy unfolded.

[1]Editor's Introduction, *WJE* 13:26, footnote 6.

Admission in the *Miscellanies*

Whilst Edwards initially adopted his grandfather's practice the subject of admission to the Supper occupied his thoughts from his early ministry. This is reflected in some entries in the *Miscellanies*. The first of these, *No. 207*, dealing with confirmation was written in 1726, the year he first arrived in the Northampton and while his grandfather was still the minister. Edwards was part of a Puritan tradition that did not practice confirmation in the Anglican model, so it is perhaps somewhat surprising that he began the entry by stating that it was 'undoubtedly a gospel institution, and sacrament too.' He then added the qualification 'the sacrament of the Lord's Supper: that is the confirmation that Christ has instituted.'[2] As he made clear at the end of the entry, he completely rejected the concept of episcopal confirmation. Since the Supper was an act of confirmation, he noted that as soon as possible children 'should come and publicly make what was done in their baptism their own act by partaking of the Lord's Supper.' This confirmation was enacted when a person was admitted to the Supper 'by him who has the care of his soul.' As a person was admitted in this way, 'Christ Jesus likewise hereby confirms him, and seals over again the same covenant, and to a worthy partaker gives the seal of the Spirit.'[3] Such an admission to the Supper marked a renewal of the covenant seal of baptism. This covenant renewal was vital since baptism did not guarantee regeneration and, as he recorded in *Miscellanies No. 577*, experience had shown, 'that multitudes of such [as are baptised] show no signs of grace at all, as they come to be capable of acting in the world; and prove wicked when they grow up.'[4] There was, therefore, a need for regenerated children to own the baptismal covenant.

Edwards defined the seal of the Spirit as 'a kind of effect of the Spirit of God on the heart, which natural men, while such, are so far from a capacity of being the subjects of, that they can have no manner of notion or idea of it.'[5] If such sealing occurred through participation in the Supper, then it is evident that, from an early stage, Edwards could not have been entirely comfortable with the view of the Supper as a converting ordinance.

[2] *WJE* 13:341.

[3] *WJE* 13:342.

[4] *WJE* 18:115.

[5] *WJE* 2:231.

In a series of four *Miscellanies* entries, dating from 1728, Edwards considered the subject of 'Visible Christians.' The issue of visible sainthood was one which first appeared in England as some within the Puritan movement began to despair of further reform of the Church of England. This led them to advocate the idea of a pure church, and to move in the direction of Separatism in an effort to put into practice 'the principles which other Puritans only held in speculation.'[6] The Separatist John Robinson, who pastored many of those in the Netherlands who would later make their way to New England, argued that the church should consist of those who were 'visibly, and so far as men in charity could judge, justified, sanctified, and entitled to the promises of salvation, and eternal life.'[7] Although the churches of New England emerged from the non-separating Puritan tradition, they soon surpassed the Separatist churches of the Old World in their application of the principle of visible sainthood and, as Edmund Morgan states, 'sometime during the 1630's the churches of New England, by introducing tests of saving faith, carried the restriction of church membership to its fullest articulation and development.'[8] As Strange has noted, the focus on visible saints gave rise to 'the whole question that had bedeviled New England almost from the beginning: Who is a visible saint and how is visible sainthood to be discerned.'[9] It was against this background that Edwards turned his attention to the subject.

In his first entry on the subject, *No. 335,* Edwards noted that if a person was a member of the church, then they ought to be a visible Christian and 'should appear so in the eye of a Christian judgment.' He said that such judgement was a public judgement which should not be undermined by the judgement of a particular individual who may know of some failure on the part of this person. Rather, 'to be a visible Christian is to appear to be a real Christian in the eye of a public Christian judgment, and to have a right in Christian reason and according to Christian rules to be received and treated as such.'[10] This reflected the concept of being a 'visible Christian' that went back to the English Separatists who, as Morgan states 'concerned themselves with outward, visible behavior and with openly expressed opinions, not with

[6] Morgan, *Visible Saints,* 32.

[7] Morgan, *Visible Saints,* 57.

[8] Morgan, *Visible Saints,* 63.

[9] Strange, "Edwards on Visible Sainthood", 99.

[10] *WJE* 13:411.

the presence or absence of saving faith.'[11] On the one hand, the terms of admission leaned towards strictness, while, on the other, judgement was to be charitable and connected to outward, discernible behaviour, rather than attempting to peer into the condition of the soul.

Edwards linked this entry to a second *No. 338* which was a more substantial reflection that wrestled in some detail with the question of who may be regarded as a visible Christian. He began by noting that persons must be treated either as Christians or not as Christians, 'there is no medium.' Yet, discerning whether they were Christians was not necessarily straightforward. In terms of private judgement, there may be no positive reason to believe that a person is a Christian, yet there may at the same time be no particular reason for people to judge that they were not a Christian and, therefore, they must be accepted as such. As a result, 'there may therefore be reason for our treating some persons as true Christians, that we have no particular reason to determine that they are so.'[12]

That was not to say that the church should neglect its duty to 'discriminate true Christians from others' by employing 'the strictest trials.' Yet, in using such trials, the church must be careful not 'to shut out multitudes that are true Christians.' To avoid this the church should apply 'Gospel rules', which were the rules given to it by Christ. The particular rule that Edwards had in mind was 'to receive those that make a profession of a hearty believing the truth of the gospel, and a walking in all the ordinances and according to the moral rules of the gospel.' In doing so he ruled out 'an examination of their particular experiences, of their discoveries, illuminations, and affections.'[13] Historically, such an examination had been part of the admission process of the New England churches, but it was one that Edwards eschewed, as did his grandfather Stoddard. Stoddard had said admission should be based on 'an Assent unto, & Acknowledgement of the Doctrine of Faith & Repentance (as the onely Doctrine according to which they hope for Salvation) together with a Promise of Obedience to all the Commandments of God.'[14] Crucially, Edwards thought that more than assent was needed and that a person should offer a 'profession of a hearty believing the truth of the gospel.'[15]

[11]Morgan, *Visible Saints,* 47.

[12]*WJE* 13:413.

[13]*WJE* 13:413.

[14]Davis and Jeske, "Stoddard's 'Arguments' ", 84.

[15]*WJE* 13:413.

In part, his rejection of a scheme of examination was based on his own conversion experience which did not conform to the classic preparationist model. As he later concluded in *Miscellanies* No. 899 'The methods of grace are obscure, as those of nature... The manner of the formation of Christ in the soul, is as indiscernible as the formation of a child, or the manner of Christ's conception in the womb of the Virgin, both which are fearful and wonderful.'[16] The problem with subjecting potential communicants to recounting their conversion was that this might shut out many who were real Christians, but whose experience did not conform to a specific pattern. This view was later confirmed by what he witnessed of conversions during the Great Awakening and then examined so carefully in *Religious Affections*. As he explained there 'Nothing can certainly be determined concerning the nature of the affections by this, that comforts and joys seem to follow awakenings and convictions of conscience, in a certain order.'[17] Even when Edwards later sought to apply stricter terms for admission to the Supper, he did not fall back on the older model of recounting conversion experiences.

He also considered the important text of Matthew 13:29, "Lest while ye gather up the tares, ye root up the wheat with them." This parable had a long history of being used in Reformed churches to explain that the church on earth must always be a mixed multitude until Christ's return. It was incumbent, therefore, upon churches not to try to separate the wheat and the tares before then. Calvin, who adopted this approach, quoted Cyprian in this respect, 'let no one arrogate to himself what is peculiar to the Son alone, and think himself sufficient to winnow the floor and cleanse the chaff, and separate all the tares by human judgment.'[18] In similar vein, Edwards commented on the text that 'Christ is very careful that wheat is not excluded.' Once again, he was expressing his concern about real Christians being unnecessarily rejected. To be a visible Christian a person must simply accept the gospel, which meant 'believing the reality of the gospel salvation and believing the necessity and sufficiency of Christ as a Savior, and other doctrines upon which these directly depend, 'tis saving faith truly to believe these.'[19] This, for Edwards, was the gospel rule received from Christ. It also confirmed his view that visible Christians were also putatively real Christians, a matter that he emphasized in the later controversy.

[16] *WJE* 20:156.

[17] *WJE* 2:151.

[18] Calvin, *Institutes,* IV. i.19.

[19] *WJE* 13:413.

The third linked entry on the subject came in *No. 345*. This was a shorter entry with a particular focus on the element of visibility. He wrote 'outwardly a Christian is to have outward faith, that is, the profession of faith, and outward holiness in the visible life and conversation.' Yet, he was still cautious and added that a person should be treated as good and honest until 'they proved otherwise.' The initial judgement was to be based upon 'hearing a good report of them as to their conversation.'[20] His fourth entry in this series, *No. 377*, briefly noted that 'Explicitly professing Christianity and the covenant of grace is the duty of everyone.' He pointed out that this, according to Scripture, 'is part of instituted religion.'[21] It is apparent from these entries that Edwards wrestled with the question of visible sainthood from early in his ministry. It was a question that, not only, touched upon salvation, but on the whole matter of church order and, particularly, who should be admitted to the Lord's Supper. It is also demonstrable from the *Miscellanies* that he was inclined towards the enactment of a charitable judgement based upon outwardly visible behaviour. Unlike, Stoddard he thought of visibility not only as outward conformity but as a sign of inward reality.

Edwards returned to the theme of visible Christians in 1730 in *Miscellanies No. 462*. Here he said that 'none should be admitted to any church privilege, to have their children baptized, or to be looked upon as of the visible church of Christ, but those that come to the Lord's Supper.'[22] It was a line of argument that he picked up again in the *Humble Inquiry* that only real Christians should come to the Lord's Supper and, therefore, only such real Christians should offer their children for baptism. As this entry suggested parents who offered their children for baptism must endeavour to ensure that they were real Christians and that their children were raised to be real Christians. In this regard they 'must examine and prove themselves, whether or no they believe the gospel with all their hearts.'[23] This examination consisted of discovering 'the Scripture evidence or visibility of Christianity to ourselves; and in the outward appearances of them, the visibility of Christianity to others.'[24] Visible evidence included forsaking all sin, universal obedience to Christ's commands, perseverance through opposition and a

[20] *WJE* 13:418.

[21] *WJE* 13:448.

[22] *WJE* 13:503.

[23] *WJE* 13:503.

[24] *WJE* 13:504.

charitable disposition to one's neighbours. While Edwards noted the need for such examination, he also bore in mind those with a sensitive conscience. People should examine themselves in light of such universal evidence and not 'the sensible exercises of grace' which might ebb and flow.[25] Again, he was keen not to exclude anyone who had a right to the Supper.

He continued that as adults tended to their own spiritual welfare, and that of their children, their aim should be to bring children to the truth of the gospel, so that in adulthood they would then join the church, knowing that only real Christians can enjoy its privileges. Those who refused to do so, because they refused to forsake all sin and fulfil all duties, condemned themselves. Again, however, he showed an awareness of the scrupulous conscience and the weakness of human nature, when he noted that those who examined themselves before the sacrament might discover a great deal of hypocrisy there. This should not put such a person off attending, but it should be an occasion for 'an immediate turning to God with more full determination, and without reserve, and without suffering any competitor in their hearts with God and religion.' Those who examined themselves and found some reservations should come 'though they are not certain.'[26] This approach to the Supper had a long history amongst the Puritans. William Ames, for example, had written that 'A worthy disposition doth not consist in perfection which if we had it, there were less need of this Sacrament: but in a sutabelnesse of our affections to so holy action; which sutabelnesse may consist with great imperfection.'[27]

For Edwards if people understood what it meant to be real Christians, and that only real Christians could participate beneficially in the church's ordinances, then the distinction between them and wicked persons would be much greater. This in turn would make those who were not real Christians much more easily targeted by the gospel as the distinction between them would be more clearly drawn by the preacher. Harry S. Stout comments that 'Edwards is clearly following Stoddard in seeking to make the Supper a "converting ordinance" in a very practical sense.'[28] If he was doing so, however, it was also in a more nuanced manner by encouraging his congregants to see that while only visible Christians had a right to the Supper, such visible Christians were also real Christians. This became clear as he completed the

[25]*WJE* 13:504.

[26]*WJE* 13:505.

[27]Ames, *Conscience*, Book IV, 85.

[28]Editor's Introduction, *WJE* 13:36.

entry with the pertinent comment 'If these things are to be insisted on as the terms of going to heaven, and also the terms of being in the church, such instructions are easy and natural to the understandings of children.'[29] Only those who had a hope of heaven had a right to the Supper, therefore, everyone should seek the conversion which meant that they had obtained a true right to the sacrament.

Edwards linked this entry to *Miscellanies No. 873* 'CONCERNING THE PROFESSION PERSONS OUGHT TO MAKE EXPLICITLY WHEN THEY COME INTO THE VISIBLE CHURCH.' The essence of this profession was that 'They ought to promise to walk in away (sic.) of obedience to all the commandments, as long as they live.'[30] Edwards then adduced numerous Old Testament passages to confirm this is what God demanded of his people, concluding that this was 'a profession consequent on conversion, and that which shall be the fruit of a glorious work of the Spirit of God in converting sinners.' He continued that they ought to profess repentance 'because their very baptism, the ordinance by which they enter into the church, does especially signify it.'[31] Furthermore, they should 'profess their faith in Jesus Christ, including a credible profession of the Christian religion.' Once more he connected such a profession to the meaning of baptism, since this was what it meant to be baptized into Christ. He continued 'for the notion of baptism is a rite of initiation into the Christian religion, and their being baptized in the name of Christ signifies this. And they ought to profess sincere, real faith or an hearty embracing [of] Christ, and reliance upon him as the Savior.'[32] As with the earlier entry, such a profession was ultimately a declaration of 'those things that are the proper qualifications and conditions of glory.'[33] From this entry, which probably dates from 1741, it is evident that Edwards was thinking about the importance of a real Christian profession as the basis for admission to the Supper before the first public adumbrations of his change of position appeared in the *Religious Affections* in 1746.[34]

[29] *WJE* 13:506.

[30] *WJE* 20:112.

[31] *WJE* 20:113.

[32] *WJE* 20:114.

[33] *WJE* 20:115.

[34] For the dating of these entries see Editor's Introduction, *WJE* 20:36, 38.

Admission in Edwards' Sermons

When Edwards succeeded his grandfather as pastor it is not surprising that he continued with the existing admissions policy given that he revered Stoddard and that the old pastor was held in such esteem in Northampton. He also followed his grandfather in a style of preaching that was designed to awaken sinners to their need. As Minkema states, regarding an early sermon on Luke 16:24, *The Torments of Hell Are Exceeding Great*, it 'shows that Edwards has learned well the terror rhetoric so successfully employed by his grandfather.'[35] In the sermon Edwards highlighted the danger of those who did not openly profess faith that they 'oftentimes secretly flatter themselves that it may be hell is not so dreadful a place as ministers pretend it is.'[36] He further warned them, they also flattered themselves that they 'shall some way or other find means to escape.' He then added 'yet you live in the neglect of means; you flatter yourself unreasonably, think to escape hell by means, and yet use no means. You think it may be that though you don't use means now, yet you intend to before long. But for all your intentions, 'tis exceeding uncertain whether you will ever escape hell.'[37] There is perhaps a hint in this statement that, initially, Edwards accepted that the Lord's Supper could act as a converting ordinance, although he added, rather skeptically, 'But for all your intentions, 'tis exceeding uncertain whether you will ever escape hell.'[38]

In a sermon preached in 1729, not long after Stoddard's death, Minkema notes, that while Edwards praised 'the memory of his grandfather by imitating his style'[39] there were also indications that he was beginning to address his pastoral legacy. His grandfather might have been held in high regard, but the town had grown spiritually careless under his leadership. Edwards' text was Jeremiah 6:29.30, 'The bellows are burnt, the lead is consumed of the fire; the founder melteth in vain: for the wicked are not plucked away. Reprobate silver shall men call them, because the Lord rejected them.' He challenged the townspeople about remaining unconverted despite living for so long under 'eminent means of conversion.' The 'eminent means' to which he referred was Stoddard and, particularly, his preaching. He remarked that

[35] Editor's Introduction, *WJE* 14:297.

[36] *WJE* 14:303.

[37] *WJE* 14:324, 325.

[38] *WJE* 14:325.

[39] Editor's Introduction, *WJE* 14:357.

'God sent Mr. Stoddard to this place because he had an elect people here, and he continued him till he had done the work his Master designed him for. Many have been gathered in by his ministry, and it looks darkly upon you that are left, especially you that have lived unconverted a long while under his ministry.'[40] The reality was, while God had sent Stoddard, the people had become hardened to his preaching and had become 'sermon proof.'[41] There was a real danger now that God would give them up to the hardness of their hearts. For 'it would be very just if he should resolve that none of you who have stood out against the calls and warnings of your former minister should have any benefit of it.'[42]

While his particular focus was the resistance of the townspeople to his grandfather's preaching, it is not too much a stretch of the imagination to suggest that he also had in mind the other means of grace, including the sacraments.[43] This would have been the case, especially, if he already held reservations about Stoddard's views about admission to the Lord's Supper, and its use as a converting ordinance. His warning to those who 'live impenitent under the most powerful and eminent means of grace, they have a great deal more to answer for than others that have lived under less advantages'[44] was equally applicable for all who attended the Lord's Supper while unconverted or who ignored its message. To neglect God's means of grace was an act of provocation directed towards God.

The carelessness of the congregation was a theme Edwards took up again in late 1729 in a sacramental sermon on Isaiah 45:25, 'In the Lord shall all the seed of Israel be justified and shall glory.' He explained that 'spiritual Israel' was the true seed of Abraham, and 'Israel was a typical nation; they were a type of the invisible church, the true people of Jesus Christ in all ages.' Having stated the doctrine, 'The people of Jesus Christ have great cause to glory in their Savior' he then posed the question 'Who are meant by the people of Christ?' His first response to the question was 'Not all those that are called Christians, or are his professed and visible people.' While many people across the world called themselves Christians, in distinction from heathens, Jews and Muslims, 'Christ's flock is but small in comparison

[40] *WJE* 14:368,369.

[41] *WJE* 14:365.

[42] *WJE* 14:369.

[43] Jamieson, "Change of Position", 128, states that this sermon 'upholds Stoddard's communion position.' The sermon does not, however, address any means of grace apart from preaching.

[44] *WJE* 14:358.

of [these]: they are but a handful; they are but thinly sown here and there in the Christian world.'[45] It was a familiar theme for him about what it meant to be a real Christian.

For Edwards real Christians were those whose hearts have been given to Christ. While the Christian world gave the appearance of belonging to Christ 'God looks at the heart, and they only are indeed the people of Jesus Christ and of his flock that have given their hearts to him and serve him.'[46] As such, they glory in Christ having a 'humble and joyful sense of mind of the great privilege and happiness they have above others in the interest they have in Christ.'[47] This was something that they could not help but declare, doing so in their behaviour, in song and, he added, 'particularly at the Lord's Supper.' This was because the Supper was 'designed partly for this end, that we might, by celebrating this ordinance, give testimony of our sense of our own happiness.'[48] He then explained that a Christian should glory in Christ, in their dependence upon him and in his name and for his honour.

As the sermon came to its application, he issued a warning to those who were hypocrites, who prided themselves in belonging to a distinct Christian party or who trusted in their natural advantages. His concluding exhortation was that they should 'Particularly endeavor that you may attend on this ordinance of the Lord's Supper with the spirit of true glory.'[49] To do so it was necessary to be assured of an interest in Christ. While Edwards continued with the admission policy of his grandfather, it is clear from this sermon that the Supper, rightly practiced, was something from which only real Christians, who gloried in Christ, could benefit. He was far from being at the point he would reach more than a decade later of arguing that only those who could profess their experience of a work of God's grace should be admitted to the Supper, but here was an indication, for those who wished to see it, that he believed from very early in his ministry that the sacrament was only of benefit to real Christians.

He adopted an even more strident tone in a sermon on Jeremiah 42:20, from the same period, 'for ye dissembled in your hearts, when ye sent me unto the Lord your God, saying, Pray for us unto the Lord our God; and according unto all that the Lord our God shall say, so declare unto

[45] *WJE* 14:461.

[46] *WJE* 14:462.

[47] *WJE* 14:463.

[48] *WJE* 14:464.

[49] *WJE* 14:469.

us, and we will do it.'[50] From this verse he established the doctrine, 'That Spiritual Calamities Are the Most terrible that Can befall a People.' Initially, he addressed those who appeared to do their Christian duty, yet they only did so with certain reservations and when it coincided with their own interests. Such people he declared 'do nothing but dissemble.' He followed this with the statement of a second doctrine, 'That there Are Some men do Nothing but dissemble in their Pretences of Disposedness to their duty.' He pointed out that such people only fulfilled their duties for the sake of public appearance and the necessary civic good. They had no regard for those duties which related to an unseen world. He noted that 'there [are] but few that Are Really disposed to do their duty.' He then remarked how such people adopted a pretence, not only in their duties, but in their prayer and in their attendance upon the ordinances. He exclaimed that of all such pretending 'the most Gross & horrid dissimulation is men's dissembling at the Lord's supper.' The Supper had been appointed for the renewal of the covenant and those who took part in it 'vow that they will be the Lords & that they set their hand & seal to the Covenant.' As they did so they 'take the body & blood of Christ in token that they will take Christ for their Lord & saviour and that they will obey his Commandments.' As such they could not be more earnest in their promise 'if they swore it by never so solemn an Oath.' Yet, between celebrations of the Supper some lived such careless lives that 'they are Guilty of the most horrid Profanation of sacred things. They are Guilty of the blood of Christ.' In an image he used frequently, he said that such people will be 'will be looked upon as some of his Crucifiers' and they 'Eat & drink Judgment to themselves.'

In his application of the sermon, he turned to exhortations and warnings, including the warning, 'Let those that have been at the sacrament today Consider whether or no you hant horribly dissembled in your Coming to Partake of Christ that ordinance and Pretending to Give yourself [to] Renew your Covenant with God & Jesus Christ.' Again, Edwards' understanding of the Supper, and his warnings against dissimulation, sit at odds with the idea that he was entirely comfortable with the practice of seeing the Supper as a converting ordinance for nominal Christians. At best, some of those who claimed that by taking part in the Supper they were sealing their baptismal covenant, were in fact doing so falsely. As such they were acting like Christ's executioners and heaping judgement on themselves.

[50]No. 094. Jeremiah 42:20, *WJEO* 43.

In another sermon from his early years Edwards was explicit that those who came to the Supper with the wrong attitude did not profit from the Supper. His text on this occasion was James 3:16, 'For where envying and strife is, there is confusion and every evil work.' While, as Valeri points out, it was preached against the background of social and economic strains in Northampton[51] it was nonetheless a sermon that focused its final point of application upon the sacrament. From the text he established the doctrine 'Envying and contention are things of exceeding pernicious consequences.' He then went on to discuss the nature of envy as an attitude of being grieved by another's prosperity. The real problem emerged, however, when this attitude would then 'break out into outward actions'[52] especially when envy gave rise to contention. In this way envy was self-destructive, as well as being harmful to the wider society. More importantly, it was also harmful to the church, where it 'exceedingly hinders the success of ordinances and the flourishing of religion amongst a people.' Such contention drove away the Spirit of God, admitted the devil and meant that 'Christ won't be in the midst of 'em.'[53]

In the application he began by addressing the theme of self-examination. He exhorted his hearers to examine themselves 'whether or no you don't harbor within yourself an envious spirit towards any of your neighbors.'[54] They then must consider whether this led to envious words or deeds. He followed this by way of reproof pointing out in great detail 'how exceeding contrary such a spirit and practice is to the spirit of Christianity.'[55] In his eleventh point of reproof he dealt with the implications for the Lord's Supper. He stated 'How exceeding unbecoming is this of those that sit at the same table of the Lord! This feast is a feast of love; Christ instituted this ordinance partly that his disciples, by coming and sitting together at the same table, might testify and seal their charity and peace with all their brethren.' A person who participated in the Lord's Supper and had envy in their heart, he pointed out, brought leaven to the sacrament, and thus voided it in the same way in which leaven had invalidated the Passover. Furthermore, he added, 'he that partakes of the Lord's Supper indulging of envy and malice in his heart, he eats and drinks judgment to himself.' He concluded,

[51]Editor's Introduction, *WJE* 17:101,102.

[52]*WJE* 17:107.

[53]*WJE* 17:110.

[54]*WJE* 17:111.

[55]*WJE* 17:115.

> How does it seem to see a company and family of the visible children of the Most High God, sitting together at God's table, feeding on the body and blood of Jesus Christ, God's own Son, who was from God's love to 'em slain to make a feast for them, and one sitting in one place envying another that sits at the same table because he gets money or because of an honorable title, and all the while having designs in his heart against him? Can you think that such sacraments are acceptable to God, and to the Lord Jesus Christ, the holy Lamb of God? No; they are abominable to him as the vomit of a dog![56]

While his words were applicable to real Christians who harboured envy, with all its insidious effects on church and society, it again poses the question of whether his statements were fully compatible with the concept of the Supper as a converting ordinance. In Edwards' view Christ was especially present in the sacrament which, as he noted here, was a seal of charity and peace among the brethren. Yet, Christ could be driven from the sacrament where envy and contention were present. This was the leaven which voided the sacrament. If this was the case it is difficult to conceive that he was comfortable with the idea that those who were not real Christians, and remained unrepentant of their sins, could take part in the Supper since that would, potentially, nullify its celebration.

There is some debate about when Edwards changed his position about admission to the Lord's Supper. Yet, whatever date one arrives at, the sermons from the early part of his ministry, along with the entries in the *Miscellanies*, reveal that, if he was consistent in his theology of the Lord's Supper, he could never have been completely at ease with the idea of it as a converting ordinance. As such it appears that his concerns about the question of who should participate in the sacrament ran much deeper, for much longer, than his public utterances later admitted.

The Admission Controversy

By the late 1740s tensions between Edwards and his congregation had been clear for some time. Edwards' disappointment at the spiritual decline of the town after the revival, the fallout from the 'young folks' Bible case and strains over his salary, all made for an uneasy relationship. It was also in this

[56]*WJE* 17:120.

period that he sought 'to launch his conservative revolution'[57] through the introduction of a new church covenant and advocating a more Presbyterian model for dealing with cases of church discipline. It was, however, his newly expressed views on admission to the Lord's Supper that brought all the simmering tensions to the boil and led to the final breakdown between minister and congregation.

Edwards' changed position on admission finally became public in 1749. In December 1748, an earnest young man approached Edwards seeking full church membership; he was the first to do so for several years. Edwards examined him according to the common standards established by his grandfather, that he adhered to orthodox Christian beliefs, that he was morally upright and that his life was devoid of scandal. By this time if Edwards had not reached a final decision on the matter, he was certainly disposed to believe that those seeking membership of the church should also offer a credible and visible profession of true godliness. This was not the step-by-step account of God's dealings with the soul, as required by the New England Way in the previous century. Rather, it was 'that they profess the great things wherein Christian piety consists, viz. a supreme respect to God, faith in Christ, etc.'[58] He enquired if the young man could offer such a profession and he agreed to think about it.

News of Edwards' new approach to admission soon spread throughout Northampton creating great unease. Such was the widespread concern about the matter that in February 1749 Edwards asked the council of the church if he might preach on the subject. They denied him this opportunity but agreed that he might publish something. He duly set about writing this piece and it was printed a few months later as *An Humble Inquiry into the Rules of the Word of God, Concerning the Qualifications Requisite to a Complete Standing and Full Communion in the Visible Christian Church*. In a febrile atmosphere 'The controversy would drag on for more than another year, but the townspeople had made up their minds.'[59] In June 1750 Edwards was removed by an overwhelming vote of the Northampton congregation.

In considering the communion controversy Edwards' argument for his change of position is set out in the *Humble Inquiry*. This was later supplemented by his *Lectures On The Qualifications For Full Communion In The*

[57]Marsden, Jonathan Edwards, 345.

[58]*WJE* 12:180.

[59]Marsden, *Jonathan Edwards,* 347. Marsden supplies a clear account of how the controversy unfolded, 341–356.

Church Of Christ, which were given weekly over five weeks, and *Misrepresentations Corrected*, which was his response to the work the town employed Solomon Williams to write in an attempt to refute his arguments. He also compiled his own *Narrative of Communion Controversy*.[60]

Edwards began the *Humble Inquiry* by posing the question 'whether, according to the rules of Christ, any ought to be admitted to the communion and privileges of members of the visible church of Christ in complete standing, but such as are in profession, and in the eye of the church's Christian judgment, godly or gracious persons?'[61] In asking this question he noted that 'a distinction should be made between members of the visible church *in general* and members *in complete standing*.'[62] He did not wish, however, to include a discussion of the question of the relationship of infants to the church which, he noted, would take another dissertation of considerable length. His essential answer to the question about admission was that this should not be based on 'so much as a common belief that Jesus is the Messiah, or a belief of the being of a God.' Rather, it ought to be based upon 'the credible profession and visibility of these things.'[63] Edwards stressed that it was not godliness that was the qualification for admission, but 'a visibility to the eye of a Christian judgment, that is the rule of the church's proceeding.'[64] This did not suggest that where a person applied for church membership they should be given the benefit of the doubt, instead there must be 'a positive judgment, founded on some positive appearance, or visibility, some outward manifestations that ordinarily render the thing probable.'[65] This meant that,

> If any are known to be persons of an honest character, and appear to be of good understanding in the doctrines of Christianity, and particularly those doctrines that teach the grand condition of salvation, and the nature of true saving religion, and publicly and seriously profess the great and main things wherein the essence

[60]Other documents related to the controversy can be found in Dismissal and Post-Dismissal Documents, *WJEO* 38.

[61]*WJE* 12:174.

[62]*WJE* 12:175.

[63]*WJE* 12:176.

[64]*WJE* 12:177.

[65]*WJE* 12:178.

> of true religion or godliness consists, and their conversation is agreeable; this justly recommends 'em.[66]

He was clear that he was not commending a scheme 'that shall be effectual to keep all hypocrites out of the church, and for the establishing in that sense a pure church.'[67] He was not following in the path of the Separatists, where one leading minister 'Ebenezer Frothingham, declared that "a Saint of God having Divine Light shining into the Understanding, and the Love of God. . . ruling in the Soul, is also to know certainly that such and such Persons are true Converts, or the Saints of God." '[68] Rather, as Crisp comments 'His conception was of a gathered communicant membership within a mixed state church — New England's Congregationalist standing order — not a separated church.'[69] Nonetheless, for those applying for admission 'they themselves should suppose the essential things, belonging to Christian piety, to be in them.'[70] In other words, he saw the benefit less in terms of protecting the church, and more in terms of protecting the applicant from outwardly confessing a faith that did not correspond to an inward reality. His fear of hypocrisy loomed once more.

Having shown 'that none ought to be admitted to the communion and privileges of members of the visible church of Christ in complete standing, but such as are in profession and in the eye of the church's Christian judgment godly or gracious persons'[71] he then explained why this should be the case. His first argument, examined the different ways in which the terms saint, Christian and disciple are used in the Bible which led him to conclude 'it appears that the distinction of real saints and visible and professing saints is scriptural, and that the visible church was made up of these two, and that none are according to Scripture admitted into the visible church of Christ, but those who are visible and professing saints or Christians.' Indeed, as he went on to point out, Stoddard agreed and supposed 'that all who come to the Lord's Supper must be visible saints, and sometimes speaks of them as professing saints. . . And supposes that it is requisite in order to their being admitted to the communion of the Lord's Table, that they

[66] *WJE* 12:179.

[67] *WJE* 12:180.

[68] Editor's Introduction, *WJE* 12:47.

[69] Crisp, "Closing of the Table", 58.

[70] *WJE* 12:181.

[71] *WJE* 12:182.

make a personal public profession of their faith and repentance to the just satisfaction of the church.'[72] The problem arose, however, when there was an attempt to distinguish between a *real* saint and a *visible* saint, as if these two terms had no correlation. In reality, a *visible* saint was someone who offered reasonable evidence that they were a *real* saint. He noted that 'To say a man is visibly a saint, but not visibly a real saint, but only visibly a visible saint, is a very absurd way of speaking.'[73] Again, he noted that Stoddard was 'himself steadfastly of the mind, that it is requisite those be not admitted to the Lord's Supper, who don't "make a personal and public profession of their faith and repentance, to the just satisfaction of the church."' Although, Edwards added how his grandfather reconciled such things 'with the rest of his treatise, I would modestly say, I must confess myself at a loss.' In this regard he drew attention to Stoddard's statement '"by the rule that God has given for admissions, if it be carefully attended, more unconverted persons will be admitted than converted."'[74] This led Edwards to query how visible signs could be the evidence upon which a person was to be judged, while at the same time persons without such evidence would more probably be admitted.

He then dealt with the issue that persons should be judged with charity so that 'since we see nothing in their lives to make us determine, that they have not had a proper effect on their hearts, we are obliged in charity to hope, that they are real saints, or gracious persons, and to treat 'em accordingly, and so to receive 'em into the Christian church, and to its special ordinances.' Such a step presupposed that a person exhibited a gracious character while at the same time saying, 'that sanctifying grace is not a necessary qualification.' On this basis Stoddard maintained that the Supper was a converting ordinance 'as much intended for the good of the unconverted, as of the converted; even as 'tis with the preaching of the gospel.'[75] Edwards questioned why there then needed to be a charitable judgement about a person to accept them at the sacrament. After all, no such judgement was made when a person was attending the preaching of the word, which Stoddard had placed on the same standing as the Supper. He argued that, based on this approach, 'there is no need of any sort of ground for treating them as saints, in order to admitting them to the Lord's Supper, the very design of which is to make

[72] *WJE* 12:183.

[73] *WJE* 12:185.

[74] *WJE* 12:186.

[75] *WJE* 12:187.

'em saints.'[76] Instead, according to the New Testament, for a person to be admitted to the church they must make a profession of faith and exhibit behaviour that corresponds to that profession. After all, 'What is it, to be a saint by profession, but to be by profession a true saint?'[77]

This raised the further question of those who made,

> a virtual and implicit profession faith... such as their owning the Christian covenant, their owning God the Father, Son and Holy Ghost, to be their God; and by their visibly joining in the public prayers and singing God's praises there is a show and implicit profession of supreme respect to God and love to him; by joining in the public confessions, they make a show of repentance; by keeping sabbaths and hearing the Word, they make a show of a spirit of obedience; by offering to come to sacraments, they make a show of love to Christ and a dependence on his sacrifice.[78]

Edwards argued that since a person may acknowledge such things, without the least pretence that they have undergone conversion, the natural understanding of using such words to profess faith was rendered meaningless. People were in effect being asked to use a form of words to declare their agreement with something which they did not believe in their hearts. The visibility that such a person was called upon to exhibit to gain admission to the Supper, was not 'supposed to be of real saintship, discipleship, and godliness, but only another sort of real godliness, than that which belongs to those who shall finally be owned by Christ as his people, at the day of judgment.'[79] He then offered nine reasons why this distinction was a human invention before concluding 'I think it abundantly evident, that the saintship, godliness and holiness, of which, according to Scripture, professing Christians and visible saints do make a profession and have a visibility, is not any religion and virtue that is the result of common grace, or moral sincerity (as it is called) but saving grace.'[80]

He next turned his attention to why it is the duty of all adults to publicly own the covenant before being admitted to the Supper. This position, he

[76] *WJE* 12:188.

[77] *WJE* 12:189.

[78] *WJE* 12:190.

[79] *WJE* 12:192.

[80] *WJE* 12:199.

remarked, was agreeable to reason, was the practice of the churches in New England and, most importantly, it was taught in Scripture. He continued with a consideration of the manner in which people in the Old Testament publicly entered into God's covenant, which was by 'swearing into God's name.'[81] He argued that 'after Christ is come and has wrought out his great redemption, the same way of publicly professing faith in the all-sufficient and immutable God by swearing "The Lord liveth," should be continued.'[82] Having made reference to several New Testament instances where God's people were said to 'confess' their faith, which was the equivalent of the Old Testament swearing, he concluded 'I know no good reason why we should not look on oral profession and covenanting with Christ, in those who are capable of it, as much of a stated duty in the Christian church, and an institution universally pertaining to the followers of Christ, as baptism.'[83] After all, he added, there was good evidence that no-one participated in the worship of Israel who did not profess faith in this way.

Edwards explained that verbally owning the covenant was important because it was saying more than 'we understand there is such a covenant, or that we understand we are obliged to comply with it; but 'tis to profess the consent of our wills, it is to manifest that we do comply with it.'[84] While some might argue that there was a distinction between the internal and external covenant, the reality was that there is only one covenant of grace, and the difference was between those who held to it internally, and those who only held to it externally. As he added, 'the New Testament affords no more foundation for supposing two real and properly distinct covenants of grace, than it does to suppose two sorts of real Christians.'[85] As such, owning the covenant only occurred as those who were baptized expressly gave themselves to God with all their hearts. Without such ownership of the covenant 'it ceases to be a profession of giving themselves up to God, and so ceases to be a professed covenanting with God, or owning God's covenant; for the thing which they profess, belongs to no covenant of God, in being.'[86] The only way in which a person could own the covenant of grace, was to do so internally as they embraced it from the heart. Otherwise, 'For persons

[81] *WJE* 12:200.

[82] *WJE* 12:202.

[83] *WJE* 12:203.

[84] *WJE* 12:205.

[85] *WJE* 12:206.

[86] *WJE* 12:207.

merely to promise, that they will believe in Christ, or that they will hereafter comply with the conditions and duties of the covenant of grace, is not to own that covenant.'[87] Instead, it became a licence for a person to delay and to continue to live in rebellion towards God. Edwards noted that, as things currently stood, people were being asked to visibly accept that which, in reality, they rejected. New England was in danger of adopting a form of outward conformity reminiscent of the Church of England.[88]

He then asserted that he could see 'no good reason why the people of Christ should not openly profess a proper respect to him in their hearts, as well as a true notion of him in their heads, or a right opinion of him in their judgments.'[89] After all, esteeming God from the heart, and not merely holding right notions about him, was the true design of religion. The reality was that 'those who live in a rejection of Christ, under the light of the gospel, and the knowledge and common belief of its doctrine, have vastly greater sin and guilt than other men.'[90] He went on to argue that there was a great battle raging between God and Satan for the hearts of the people. In this struggle there could be no middle way, a person either gave themselves to God with an undivided heart, or they sided with his rival.

He next pointed out that those who professed to be visible saints, and yet were not truly godly, were known in Scripture as 'counterfeits' or 'hypocrites.'[91] He added that in several places Stoddard concurred with this view. Yet, Edwards wondered how these visible saints could be accused of hypocrisy 'when they never made a pretense to anything more than common grace, or moral sincerity, which many of them truly have.'[92] A person can only be accused of hypocrisy if they have made a profession of loving God from the heart but have acted in a contrary manner. When God accused his people in the Old Testament of hypocrisy, it was because when they professed to be his visible people it was at the same time a profession of true godliness.

He then considered the transition between the old covenant and the new. He pointed out that when the Old Testament looked forward to the new age and the admission of the Gentiles it was for 'the great qualification, which

[87] *WJE* 12:209.

[88] *WJE* 12:213.

[89] *WJE* 12:219.

[90] *WJE* 12:220.

[91] *WJE* 12:221.

[92] *WJE* 12:222.

should be looked at in those blessed days, when these external ceremonial qualifications of circumcision and soundness of body should no more be insisted on, viz. piety of heart and practice. "Joining themselves to the Lord, loving the name of the Lord, to be his servants, choosing the things that please him," etc.'[93] On turning to the New Testament it was 'manifest that all visible Christians or saints, all Christ's professing disciples or hearers that profess him to be their Lord, according to the Scripture notion of professing Christ, are such as profess a saving interest in him and relation to him, and live in the hope of being hereafter owned as those that are so interested and related.'[94] This accounted for Christ's words in Matthew 7:22,23, where he said he would ultimately dismiss those who cry to him 'Lord! Lord' with the words 'I never knew you'. They could only be discharged in this way if they believed that their visible behaviour represented a real relationship with Christ. This same teaching was reiterated by Jesus at numerous places in the Gospels, such as the parable of the Ten Virgins in Matthew 25. Throughout the Gospels visible Christians were those who believed they had a real interest in Christ.

Edwards argued that this point was further reinforced by turning to consider the life of the early church in the book of Acts. Here people had to make a profession to gain admittance to the church. This profession was that they had repented and believed in the Lord Jesus for salvation. He asked if it was then reasonable to believe that any who made such a profession 'had any such distinction in view as that which some now make of two sorts of real Christianity, two sorts of sincere faith and repentance, one with a moral and another with a gracious sincerity.'[95] An examination of the church after Pentecost in Acts 2, made it clear that those who were added to the church believed themselves to be in a right standing with God. This pattern of believing the gospel, followed by admission to the church, was one repeated throughout Acts. Moving on to the epistles it was again clear that the apostles treated all those whom they addressed as true believers. This was,

> how all the Christian churches through the world were constituted in those days; and what sort of holiness or saintship it was, that all visible Christians in good standing had a visibility

[93] *WJE* 12:224.

[94] *WJE* 12:226.

[95] *WJE* 12:231.

> and profession of, in that apostolic age; and also what sort of visibility of this they had, viz. not only that which gave 'em right to a kind of negative charity, or freedom from censure, but that which might justly induce a positive judgment in their favor.[96]

Edwards' next line of argument focused on one of his favourite themes that 'the Scripture represents the visible church of Christ, as a society having its several members united by the bond of Christian brotherly love.'[97] This love was more than a general sense of benevolence or charity. Rather, it represented 'a peculiar and very distinguishing kind of affection, that every true Christian experiences towards those whom he looks upon as truly gracious persons.'[98] Such sincere love could only be expected amongst Christians where they believed that their fellow Christians are truly united to them as part of God's family. With this in mind, he observed 'how eminently fit and proper for this purpose is the sacrament of the Lord's Supper, the Christian church's great feast of love; wherein Christ's people sit together as brethren in the family of God, at their father's table, to feast on the love of their Redeemer, commemorating his sufferings for them, and his dying love to them, and sealing their love to him and one another?'[99]It was scarcely believable that Christ would have instituted such an act of worship for his people and then expected them to enter into it with a group of people, the majority of whom remained unconverted.

In the final section of the work Edwards considered the Supper more directly. He stated that 'It is necessary, that those who partake of the Lord's Supper, should judge themselves truly and cordially to accept of Christ, as their only Savior and chief Good.' This was necessary because 'this is what the actions, which communicants perform at the Lord's Table, are a solemn profession of.' The Lord's Supper, he explained, was a covenant renewal ceremony in which the presiding minister stood in Christ's place. In this way 'Christ, by the speeches and actions of the minister, makes a solemn profession of his part in the covenant of grace.' Those who received the bread and wine then professed their part in the covenant. In doing so, 'they profess to embrace the promises and lay hold of the hope set before them, to receive the atonement, to receive Christ as their spiritual food, and to

[96]*WJE* 12:245.

[97]*WJE* 12:251.

[98]*WJE* 12:252.

[99]*WJE* 12:255.

feed upon him in their hearts by faith.' Notably, 'what is professed on both sides is the heart: for Christ, in offering himself, professes the willingness of his heart to be theirs who truly receive him; and the communicants, on their part, profess the willingness of their hearts to receive him, which they declare by significant actions.'[100] The actions undertaken in the Supper have all the solemnity of words that have been spoken. Consequently, for people 'solemnly to profess that which at the same time they don't at all imagine they experience in themselves, and don't really pretend to, is a very great absurdity.'[101]

He then considered the important text 1 Corinthians 11:28 on self-examination. This command involved a person examining themselves regarding their having experienced a true work of grace. It did not mean, as some had argued, that a person should examine themselves considering the deficiencies that they bring to the sacrament. Rather, it 'properly signifies "proving" or "trying" a thing with respect to its quality and goodness, or in order to determine whether it be true and of the right sort.'[102] Edwards noted that this was how William Ames and Samuel Willard[103] understood the word 'examine.' He offered several texts from the New Testament to support this. He also rejected the interpretation of the text that argued Paul was calling upon the Corinthians to examine whether there was any scandal in their lives, rather than whether they were true believers. He further rejected as absurd the claim that what 'the Apostle would have them examine themselves about, is, whether they have doctrinal knowledge, sufficient to understand, that the bread and wine in the sacrament signify the body and blood of Christ.' This would only make sense if Paul, in all the time he had spent among the Corinthians, had failed to explain to them the significance of the bread and wine. Instead, Paul's exhortation was directed towards,

> he that has no spiritual taste wherewith to perceive anything more at the Lord's Supper, than common food; or that has no higher view, than with a little seeming devotion to eat bread, as it were in the way of an ordinance, but without regarding in his heart the spiritual meaning and end of it and without

[100] *WJE* 12:256.

[101] *WJE* 12:258.

[102] *WJE* 12:258.

[103] Samuel Willard (1640–1707) was a New England minister who for a time acted as president of Harvard.

> being at all suitably affected with the dying love of Christ therein commemorated.'[104]

He remarked that, ultimately, 'It's only a living faith that capacitates men to discern the Lord's body in the sacrament with that spiritual sensation or spiritual gust, which is suitable to the nature and design of the ordinance, and which the Apostle seems principally to intend.'[105] These arguments formed the principal case by which Edwards reasoned that a person should only be admitted to full standing in the church if they were able to profess a work of God's grace in their lives. In the rest of the work Edwards dealt with various objections to his view.

Edwards' *Lectures on Communion* were delivered in early 1750 and, inevitably, they covered some of the same ground as his *Humble Inquiry*. As Kimnach comments 'While the conceptual burden of the two works is the same insistence upon a sincere profession of godliness as a prerequisite to complete standing in the church, the treatise is primarily an exegetical argument from Scripture.'[106] Over the course of twenty-two arguments Edwards defended his views concluding with a sweeping overview of the New Testament where he stated,

> 'Tis apparent by the account the New Testament gives us, that all the churches in the world in the apostles' days were in fact so constituted as is represented in the doctrine; i.e. that all the members of all the Christian church through the face of the whole earth at that day, were admitted under no other notion than as being real saints, on their being so by profession and in the eye of a reasonable judgment.

It was the essence of his argument in all the writings on the Communion Controversy that visible saints should be admitted to the Supper on the basis that they professed to be real saints. It is evident from what has been seen in earlier chapters that many of the arguments Edwards put forward in works produced during the controversy were, at the very least, implicit in his theology of the Lord's Supper long before he was forced to defend his views in the late 1740s.

[104] *WJE* 12:260.

[105] *WJE* 12:262.

[106] Editor's Introduction, *WJE* 25:349, 350.

The Change of Position

When exactly Edwards changed his position about admission is still a matter of some debate. As Jamieson states 'It is clear that even in 1738 he had begun to consider the implications for church polity of the revival phenomena and of Calvinism.'[107] Certainly his views had, it seems, changed by 1745. Ola Winslow states that 'many of his brother ministers and many in his own congregation knew of his changed view, and by 1745 it was an open secret.'[108] Hall has written 'The evidence suggests that he had changed his mind by 1745 or when he began writing the *Religious Affections*. The evidence also suggests that he was in no hurry to inform his congregation.'[109] In his *Narrative* of the events surrounding his dismissal, Edwards wrote, 'I also designedly gave some intimations of my notions of visible Christians in my work on *Religious Affections*, but was aware that when I came to be necessitated to act upon my principles, and on this footing decline admitting any who should offer themselves to be received to communion, this would occasion a more general noise and tumult.'[110] This timescale was later confirmed by Joseph Bellamy, James Pierpont, Noah Parsons, John Searle, and his wife, Sarah Edwards, in a series of depositions made in 1750.[111]

Why Edwards chose to make his position public when he did is perhaps more difficult to uncover. The views that he began to express publicly had long been woven into his thinking about the Supper. Indeed, in Danaher's words 'The question no longer is merely what made Edwards change his mind administratively, but why it took him so long to follow through the theological implications of his thought, since he conceived the Lord's Supper in terms so different from Stoddard.'[112] The fact that he traced this change of position back to the time he was writing *Religious Affections* is undoubtedly significant given that it was a work that dealt with what it meant to be a real Christian. Rightmire asserts 'The primary reason Edwards' view of the sacrament changed was not due to concerns of practicality, purity, or church polity; rather, it was due to a gradual awareness of the nature of

[107] Jamieson, "Change of Position", 94.

[108] Quoted in Jamieson, "Change of Position", 94.

[109] Editor's Introduction, *WJE* 12:53.

[110] *WJE* 12:508.

[111] "Depositions" (1750), *WJEO* 38.

[112] Danaher, "By Sensible Signs", 286.

the religious experience itself.'[113] Contemporaries were more cynical and thought that he chose his moment following the death of his uncle John Stoddard. They believed that Edwards would not have expressed his views publicly had Solomon Stoddard's son been alive to protect his father's legacy. Although, it may simply have been that the young man seeking membership in 1748 offered the first opportunity to express his new position.

There is no doubt that the return of the town to spiritual lassitude in the 1740s concerned Edwards. It is also clear that he spent a good deal of time thinking about the true nature of religious experience. Yet, caution needs to be taken in drawing too direct a line between these and the change in his position about the qualifications for communicant membership. After all, Edwards had lived through a similar period of revival followed by declension in the 1730s. This was not a completely new experience. Furthermore, the nature of true religious experience had occupied his thoughts since the 1720s. It is necessary, therefore, to consider other factors which, when combined with his concerns over spiritual laxity, may have helped to move him in the direction of change.

In the preface to *An Humble Inquiry* Edwards referred to his opinions on true religion as expressed in *Religious Affections* and his 'observations and reflections on Mr. Brainerd's life' which had been published the following year.[114] Danaher is rather dismissive of Brainerd's influence on Edwards, remarking that it seems unlikely 'Edwards gained much sacramental insight from these reflections [on the Supper].'[115] Yet, as Norman Pettit observes, while 'Edwards never once transcribed a conversation with Brainerd, any connection between the communion controversy and Brainerd'sexample in the diary ought to be considered; for the principles that Edwards upheld, Brainerd had applied in New Jersey and on the Pennsylvania frontier.'[116] Brainerd may not have been the source of Edwards' views on the Supper, but given what he said about the Supper, he may have inspired him and strengthened his resolve.

Reading Brainerd's accounts of the Supper two things appear especially relevant in connection with Edwards' position in the late 1740s. The first is the evident sense of heightened affections Brainerd experienced as he celebrated the sacrament, especially among the Scots Presbyterians. Commu-

[113]Rightmire, "Sacramental Theology", 59.

[114]*WJE* 12:171.

[115]Danaher, "By Sensible Signs", 271.

[116]Editor's Introduction, *WJE* 7:15.

nion seasons were historically times of increased devotion among Scottish Presbyterians in Scotland and Ulster. For example, among the Scottish Presbyterians in Ulster a communion season precipitated the 1625 Sixmilewater revival in County Antrim. As Eric Leigh Schmidt states 'The sacramental occasion, as one of the most prominent features of the evangelical Presbyterian tradition, was soon re-created in America.'[117] In a typical remark on his experience of such a celebration of the Supper Brainerd wrote 'At the sacrament of the Lord's Supper, seemed strong in the Lord; and the world with all its frowns and flatteries in a great measure disappeared, so that my soul had nothing to do with them; and I felt a disposition to be wholly and forever the Lord's.'[118] Such rhapsodic entries appear regularly in his diary with regard to the Supper. For example, he later wrote, 'My soul was full of love and tenderness towards the children of God, and towards all men: Felt a certain sweetness of disposition towards every creature.'[119] Among the Indians he recorded,

> The ordinance was attended with great solemnity, and with a most desirable tenderness and affection. And 'twas remarkable that in the season of the performance of the sacramental actions, especially in the distribution of the bread, they seemed to be affected in a most lively manner, as if Christ had been really crucified before them. And the words of the institution, when repeated and enlarged upon in the season of the administration, seemed to meet with the same reception, to be entertained with the same full and firm belief and affectionate engagement of soul, as if the Lord Jesus Christ himself had been present and had personally spoken to them.[120]

Pettit says that Edwards viewed Brainerd as 'a penetrating genius, of clear thought, of close reasoning, and a very exact judgment and knowledge of things in divinity, but especially in things appertaining to inward experimental religion.'[121] It seems likely, therefore, Brainerd's accounts of his experiences of the Supper reflected all that Edwards thought such a

[117]Schmidt, *Holy Fairs*, 53.

[118]*WJE* 7:192.

[119]*WJE* 7:251.

[120]*WJE* 7:386, 387.

[121]Editor's Introduction, *WJE* 7:92.

celebration should be, with affecting views of God and his people and deep experiences of Christ's presence. Edwards, however, was living through a period of spiritual drought, where some, he feared, were attending the sacrament having had no real acquaintance with the true work of the Holy Spirit in their lives. His experiences of the celebration of the Lord's Supper must have appeared far removed from those described by Brainerd.

The second matter arising from Brainerd's diary is his practice regarding preparation for and admission to the Supper. He recorded how he 'catechized those that were designed to partake of the Lord's Supper the next day, upon the institution, nature, and end of that ordinance; and had abundant satisfaction respecting their doctrinal knowledge and fitness in that respect for an attendance upon it.'[122] He noted on another occasion that he had 'apprehended that a number of persons in my congregation were proper subjects of the ordinance of the Lord's Supper, and that it might be seasonable speedily to administer it to them.' Having decided to proceed with the celebration of the Supper he then set aside a day for preparation 'for solemn fasting and prayer, to implore the blessing of God upon our design of renewing covenant with him, and with one another, to walk together in the fear of God, in love and Christian fellowship; and to entreat that his divine presence might be with us in our designed approach to his table.'[123] In a later entry Brainerd spoke of having established a society of over one hundred and sixty Indians. He noted that of 'these there are thirty-seven who have been admitted to the sacraments of baptism and the Lord's Supper, and who, in a judgment of charity, appear to have experienced a work of saving grace in their hearts.'[124]

Again, Brainerd's experience coincided with the views that Edwards had reached where the minister ought to have a prominent role in judging who was sufficiently ready to be admitted to the Supper on the grounds of their experience of God's grace. Although, it is perhaps ironic, that Brainerd's diary also records occasions where unbelievers were deeply affected by the celebration of the Supper making it a converting ordinance. He recorded on one occasion, for example, 'The religious people were affected and even melted with divine truths, with a view of the dying love of Christ. Sundry others who had been for some months under convictions of their perishing state, appeared now to be much moved with concern, and afresh engaged in

[122]*WJE* 7:386.

[123]*WJE* 7:383, 384.

[124]*WJE* 7:586.

seeking after an interest in Christ.'[125] Edwards had gone for years without a convert through the Supper and, by the time he published Brainerd's diary, it had been several years since anyone had even applied for full membership of the church. The idea that the Supper might function as a converting ordinance was far removed from the reality of its practice in Northampton.

While the publication of *Religious Affections* and Brainerd's diary may have coincided with Edwards making public his change of position it seems that its roots can be found long before the 1740s. Perhaps Edwards' most pertinent comment on whole subject came in his *Narrative* of the communion controversy when he wrote 'I have had difficulties in my mind for many years, with regard to admission of members into the church who made no pretense to real godliness.'[126] Far from Edwards' views in the 1740s representing a complete *volte-face,* what occurred was the final resolution of tension that he had lived with throughout the Northampton pastorate. As he admitted in *An Humble Inquiry,* he had hitherto conformed to Solomon Stoddard's in the administration of the sacrament 'though never without some difficulties in my view.' Why then did it take him more than twenty years to make these scruples known? Edwards explained he had 'a distrust of my own understanding, and deference to the authority of so venerable a man, the seeming strength of some of his arguments, together with the success he had in his ministry, and his great reputation and influence, prevailed for a long time to bear down my scruples.' What eventually led him to reject his grandfather's view was, he continued,

> I became more studied in divinity, and as I improved in experience; this brought me to closer diligence and care to search the Scriptures, and more impartially to examine and weigh the arguments of my grandfather, and such other authors as I could get on his side of the question. By which means, after long searching, pondering, viewing and reviewing, I gained satisfaction, became fully settled in the opinion I now maintain.[127]

While Edwards found himself torn between the views of his father and the views of his grandfather, in the end, as Marsden has commented, 'he was Timothy Edwards' son more than he was Solomon Stoddard's grandson.'[128]

[125] *WJE* 7:385.

[126] *WJE* 12:507.

[127] *WJE* 12:169, 170.

[128] Marsden, *Jonathan Edwards,* 352.

BIBLIOGRAPHY

Allen, Michael. 2016. "Sacraments in the Reformed and Anglican Reformation." In *The Oxford Handbook of Sacramental Theology*, edited by Hans Boersma and Matthew Levering, 283–297. Oxford: Oxford University Press.

Ames, William. 1639. *Conscience with the Power and Cases thereof Devided into V. Bookes. Written by the godly and learned, William Ames, Doctor, and Professor of Divinity, in the famous University of Franeker in Friesland. Translated out of Latine into English, for more publique benefit.* Leyden and London: W.Christiaens, E.Griffin, J.Dawson.

—. 1997. *The Marrow of Theology.* Translated by John Eusden. Grand Rapids, MI: Baker Books.

Baker, J. Wayne. 1998. "Heinrich Bullinger, the Covenant, and the Reformed Tradition in Retrospect." *The Sixteenth Century Journal* 356–376.

Bezzant, Rhys. 2021. "Ecclesiology and Sacraments." In *The Oxford Handbook of Jonathan Edwards*, edited by Douglas A. Sweeney and Jan Stievermann, 267–280. Oxford: Oxford University Press.

Bezzant, Rhys S. 2014. *Jonathan Edwards and the Church.* New York: Oxford University Press.

Bierma, Lyle D. 2021. *Font of Pardon and New Life : John Calvin and the Efficacy of Baptism.* New York: Oxford University Press.

Bombaro, John J. 2004. "Dispositional Peculiarity, History, and Edwards's Evangelistic Appeal to Self-Love." *Westminster Theological Journal* 121–157.

Bray, Gerald. 2014. *God Has Spoken: A History of Christian Theology.* Nottingham: Apollos.

Bromiley, Geoffrey. 1953. *Zwingli and Bullinger / Selected Translations with Introductions and Notes by G.W. Bromiley.* London : SCM Press.

Caldwell, Robert W. 2007. *Communion in the Spirit : The Holy Spirit as the Bond of Union in the Theology of Jonathan Edwards.* Eugene, OR: Wipf & Stock.

Calvin, John. 2008. *Institutes of the Christian Religion.* Translated by Henry Beveridge. Peabody, MA: Hendrickson Publishers, Inc.

Campi, Emidio. 2016. "The Consensus Tigurinus: Origins, Assessment, and Impact." *Reformation and Renaissance Review* 5–24.

Chamberlain, Ava. 1999. "Jonathan Edwards on the Relation between Hypocrisy and the Religious." In *Perspectives on American Religion and Culture,* edited by Peter W. Williams, 336–352. Edinburgh: Blackwell.

Charnock, Stephen. 1985. *A Discourse of the End of the Lord's Supper.* Vol. 4, in *The Complete Works of Stephen Charnock,* by Stephen Charnock, 392–426. Edinburgh: Banner of Truth Trust.

Cochrane, Arthur C. 1966. *Reformed Confessions of the Sixteenth Century.* Philadelphia, PA: Westminster Press.

Cotton, John. 1641. *The Way of Life, Or, Gods Way and Course, in Bringing the Soule into, Keeping it in, and Carrying it on, in the Wayes of Life and Peace Laid Downe in Foure Severall Treatises on Foure Texts of Scripture.* London: Printed by M.F. for L. Fawne and S. Gellibrand.

Cranmer, Thomas. 1825. *A Defence of the True and Catholick Doctrine of the Sacrament of the Body and Blood of our Saviour Christ : With a Confutation of Sundry Errors Concerning the Same.* London: C. and J. Rivington [et.al].

Crisp, Oliver D. 2010. "Jonathan Edwards on the Qualifications for Communion." In *Retrieving Doctrine: Essays in Reformed Theology,* by Oliver D. Crisp, 182–203. Downers Grove, IL: InterVarsity Press.

Crisp, Oliver. 2009. "Jonathan Edwards and the Closing of the Table: Must the Eucharist Be Open to All?" *Ecclesiology* 48–68.

Danaher Jr., William J. 1998. "By Sensible Signs Represented: Jonathan Edwards' Sermons on the Lord's Supper." *Pro Ecclesia* 261–287.

Davies, Horton. 1990. *The Worship of the American Puritans, 1629–1730.* New York: Peter Lang.

—. 1997. *The Worship of the English Puritans.* Morgan, PA: Soli Deo Gloria Publications.

Davis, Thomas M. and Jeff Jeske. 1976. "Solomon Stoddard's 'Arguments' Concerning Admission to the Lord's Supper." *Proceedings of the American Antiquarian Society* 75–111.

Davis, Thomas M. 1974. "Solomon Stoddard's Sermon on the Lord's Supper as a Converting Ordinance." *Resources for American Literary Study* 205–224.

Elwood, Christopher. 1999. *The Body Broken: The Calvinist Doctrine of the Eucharist and the Symbolization of Power in Sixteenth-Century France.* New York: Oxford University Press.

Euler, Carrie. 2013. "Huldrych Zwingli and Heinrich Bullinger." In *A Companion to the Eucharist in the Reformation*, edited by Lee Palmer Wandel, 57–74. Leiden: Brill.

Finch, Martha. 2009. *Dissenting Bodies: Corporealities in Early New England.* New York: Columbia University Press.

Gerrish, B.A. 1982. *The Old Protestantism and the New.* Edinburgh: T&T Clark.

Gerstner, John H. 1995. *Jonathan Edwards, Evangelist.* Morgan, PA: Soli Deo Gloria Publications.

Gray, Andrew. 1715. *The Mystery of Faith Opened Up; Or Some Sermons Concerning Faith ... Whereunto are Added Other Three Sermons, Two Concerning the Great Salvation, a Third Concerning Death ... All These Sermons Being Now Carefully Revised, and Much Corrected.* Edinburgh: Heirs and Successors of Andrew Gray.

Greenham, Richard. 1605. *The Workes of the Reuerend and Faithfull Seruant of Iesus Christ M. Richard Greenham, Minister and Preacher of the Word of God Collected into One Volume: Reuised, Corrected, and Published, for the Further Building of All Such as Loue the Trueth, and Desire to Know the Power of Godlinesse.* London: Imprinted by Felix Kyngston, for Cuthbert Burbie, and are to be solde at his shop in Paules Church-yard at the signe of the Swanne.

Greenwood, John and Henry Barrow. 1962. *The Writings of John Greenwood, 1587–1590 : Together with the Joint Writings of Henry Barrow and John Greenwood, 1587–1590.* Edited by Leland H. Carson. London: George Allen and Unwin.

Griffiths, Benjamin. 2001 . *Playing the Past: Approaches to English Historical Drama, 1385–1600.* Woodbridge: D.S. Brewer.

Hall, David D. 2008. "New England, 1660–1730." In *The Cambridge Companion to Puritanism*, edited by John Coffey and Paul C. H. Lim, 143–158. Cambridge: Cambridge University Press.

Hall, Michael G. 1988. *The Last American Puritan: The Life of Increase Mather, 1639–1723.* Hanover, NH: University Press of New England.

Hawkins, William L. 2017. "Sacraments." In *The Jonathan Edwards Encyclopedia*, edited by Harry S. Stout, 505–507. Grand Rapids, MI: Wm. B. Eerdmans Publishing Co.

Henry, Matthew. 1715. *The Communicant's Companion: Or, Instructions and Helps for the Right Receiving of the Lord's Supper. By Matthew Henry, Minister of the Gospel.* London: Printed for M. Lawrence, at the Angel in the Poultry, J. Nicholson, at the Kings-Arms, J. and B. Sprint, at the Bell in Little Britain, S. Cliffe, at the Bible and Three Crowns in Cheapside, and D. Jackson, at the Bible and Three Crowns in the Poultry.

Holifield, E. Brooks. 2016. "Sacramental Theology in America: Seventeenth–Nineteenth Centuries." In *The Oxford Handbook of Sacramental Theology*, edited by Hans Boersma and Matthew Levering, 380–395. Oxford: Oxford University Press.

—. 1974. *The Covenant Sealed : The Development of Puritan Sacramental Theology in Old and New England, 1570–1720* . New Haven, CT: Yale University Press.

Hopkins, Samuel. 1804. *The Life and Character of the Late Reverend, Learned, and Pious Mr. Jonathan Edwards, President of the College of New Jersey.* Northampton, MA: Andrew Wright.

Houston, Julia. 1994. "Transubstantiation and the Sign: Cranmer's Drama of the Lord's Supper." *Journal of Medieval and Early Modern Studies* 113–130.

Hunt, Arnold. 1998. "The Lord's Supper in Early Modern England." *Past & Present* 39–83.

Jamison, John F. 1981. "Jonathan Edwards's Change of Position On Stoddardeanism." *Harvard Theological Review* 79–99.

Jenson, Gordon A. 2014. "Luther and the Lord's Supper." In *The Oxford Handbook of Martin Luther's Theology*, edited by Robert Kolb, Irene Dingel and L'ubomir Batka, 322–331. Oxford: Oxford University Press.

Johnson, Maxwell E. 2012. *Sacraments and Worship.* Louisville, KY: Westminster John Knox.

Joo, Jong Hun. 2017. *Matthew Henry: Pastoral Liturgy in Challenging Times.* Cambridge: James Clarke and Co.

Knight, Janice. 1994. *Orthodoxies in Massachusetts: Re-Reading American Puritanism.* Cambridge, MA: Harvard University Press.

Lane, Anthony N.S. 2007. "Was Calvin a Crypto-Zwinglian?" In *Adaptations of Calvinism in Reformation Europe : Essays in Honour of Brian G. Armstrong*, edited by Mack P. Holt, 21–42. Aldershot: Ashgate.

Lane, Belden C. 2011. *Ravished by Beauty: The Surprising Legacy of Reformed Spirituality.* New York: Oxford University Press.

Leppin, Volker. 2013. "Martin Luther." In *A Companion to the Eucharist in the Reformation*, edited by Lee Palmer Wandel, 39–56. Leiden: Brill.

Lucas, Paul R. 1996. "The Death of the Prophet Lamented." In *Jonathan Edwards's Writings: Text, Context, Interpretation*, edited by Stephen J. Stein, 69–84. Bloomington, IN: Indiana University Press.

Luke, David. 2017. "Disposition." In *The Jonathan Edwards Encyclopedia*, edited by Harry S. Stout, 147–149. Grand Rapids, MI: Wm. B. Eerdmans Publishing Co.

Luke, David. 2021. *The 'reception of Christ with the faculties of the soul': Conversion in the "Miscellanies".* Vol. 2, in *The Miscellanies Companion*, edited by Robert L. Boss and Sarah B. Boss, 321–334. Fort Worth, TX: JE Society Press.

MacCulloch, Diarmaid. 1996. *Thomas Cranmer: A Life.* New Haven, CT: Yale University Press.

Marsden, George. 2003. *Jonathan Edwards: A Life.* New Haven, CT: Yale University Press.

Mastricht, Petrus Van. 1699. *Theoretico-practica Theologia, qua, per singula capita theologica, pars exegetica, dogmatica, elenchtica & practica, perpetua successione conjugantur.* Vol. 2. Utrecht: Gerardum Muntendam.

Mathison, Keith. 2017. "The Lord's Supper." In *Reformation History: A Systematic Summary*, edited by Matthew Barrett and Michael Scott Horton, 643–674. Illinois, IL: Crossway.

Mayor, Stephen. 1972. *The Lord's Supper in Early English Dissent.* Eugene, OR: Wipf & Stock.

McClymond, Michael J. 1997. "Spiritual Perception in Jonathan Edwards." *The Journal of Religion* 195–216.

McClymond, Michael J., and Gerald R. McDermott. 2012. *The Theology of Jonathan Edwards.* New York: Oxford University Press.

McDowell, David Paul. 2012. *Beyond the Half-Way Covenant: Solomon Stoddard's Understanding of the Lord's Supper as a Converting Ordinance.* Eugene, OR: Wipf & Stock.

Miller, Perry. 1959. *Jonathan Edwards.* New York: Meridian Books.

Moore, Susan Hardman. 2020. *Worship and Sacraments.* Vol. I, in *The Oxford History of Protestant Dissenting Traditions*, edited by John Coffey, 409–434. Oxford: Oxford University Press.

Morgan, Edmund S. 1965. *Visible Saints the History of a Puritan Idea.* Itacha, NY: Cornell University Press.

Muller, Richard A. 2012. *Calvin and the Reformed Tradition: On the Work of Christ and the Order of Salvation.* Grand Rapids, MI: Baker Academic.

Murdock, Graeme. 2004. *Beyond Calvin: the Intellectual, Political and Cultural World of Europe's Reformed Churches, c. 1540–1620.* Basingstoke: Palgrave Macmillan.

Neele, Adriaan C. 2018. *Before Jonathan Edwards: Sources of New England Theology*. New York:Oxford Univeristy Press.

Njoto, Ricky F. 2019. "The Lord's Supper in the Hands of a Sensitive Preacher: The Bible in Edwards' Sermons on 1 Corinthians 10." *Jonathan Edwards Studies* 28–59.

Oberman, Heiko A. 1989. *Luther: Man Between God and the Devil.* Translated by Eileen Walliser-Schwarzbart. New Haven, CT: Yale University Press.

Old, Hughes Oliphant. 2013. *Holy Communion the the Piety of the Reformed Church.* Powder Springs, GA: Tolle Lege Press.

Owen, John. 2009. *Communion with the Triune God.* Edited by Kelly M. Kapic and Justin Taylor. Wheaton, IL: Crossway Books.

Patterson, W. B. 2014. *William Perkins and the Making of a Protestant England.* Oxford: Oxford University Press.

Pauw, Amy Plantinga. 2010. "Jonathan Edwards' Ecclesiology." In *Jonathan Edwards as Contemporary: Essays in Honor of Sang Hyun Lee*, edited by Don Schweitzer, 175–186. New York: Peter Lang.

Payne, Jon D. 2004. *John Owen on the Lord's Supper.* Edinburgh: The Banner of Truth Trust.

Perkins, William. 2018. *A Golden Chain.* Vol. 6, in *The Works of William Perkins*, edited by Joel R. Beeke and Greg A. Salazar, 53–347. Grand Rapids, MI: Reformation Heritage Books.

Perkins, William. 2019. *A Reformed Catholic.* Vol. 7, in *The Works of William Perkins*, edited by Shawn D. Wright, 41–223. Grand Rapids, MI: Reformation Heritage Books.

Perkins, William. 2017. *The Foundation of Christian Religion Gathered into Six Principles.* Vol. 5, in *The Works of William Perkins*, edited by Ryan Hurd, 502–524. Grand Rapids. MI: Reformation Heritage Books.

Pettit, Norman. 1989. *The Heart Prepared:Grace and Conversion in the Puritan Spiritual Life.* 2nd. Middletown, CT: Wesleyan University Press.

Poole, Matthew. 1963. *Commentary on the Whole Bible.* Vol. 3. London: Banner of Truth Trust.

Pruett, Gordon E. 1975. "A Protestant Doctrine of the Eucharistic Presence." *Calvin Theological Journal* 142–174.

Rightmire, R. David. 1989. “The Sacramental Theology of Jonathan Edwards in the Context of Controversy.” *Fides et Historia* 50–60.

Robinson, Paul W. 2016. *The Annotated Luther.* Minneapolis, MN: Fortress Press.

Rozeboom, Sue A. 2012. “Doctrine of the Lord' Supper: Calvin's Theology and its Early Reception.” In *Calvin's Theology and its Reception: Disputes, Developments and New Possibilities*, edited by J. Todd Billings and I. John Hesselink, 143–165. Lousiville, KY: Westminster John Knox Press.

Schmidt, Eric Leigh. 2001. *Holy Fairs: Scotland and the Making of American Revivalism.* 2nd. Grand Rapids, MI: Wm. B. Eerdmans Publishing Company.

Shepard, Thomas. 1853. *The Church Membership of Children and Their Right to Baptism.* Vol. 3, in *The Works of Thomas Shepard: First Pastor of the First Church Cambridge*, by Thomas Shepard, 491–540. Boston, MA: Doctrinal Tract and Book Society.

Shepard, Thomas. 1853. *The Sum of Christian Religion in Way of Question and Answer.* Vol. 1, in *The Works of Thomas Shepard: First Pastor of the First Church, Cambridge*, by Thomas Shepard, 337–351. Boston, MA: Doctrinal Tract and Book Society.

Sibbes, Richard. 1863. *The Right Receiving.* Vol. IV, in *The Complete Works of Richard Sibbes, D.D.*, by Richard Sibbes, edited by Alexander Balloch Grossart, 61–77. Edinburgh: James Nichol.

Spinks, Bryan D. 2014. *Do this in Remembrance of Me: The Eucharist from the Early Church to the Present Day.* London: Hymns Ancient and Modern.

Stephens, W.P. 1992. *Zwingli : An Introduction to His Thought.* Oxford: Clarendon.

Stoddard, Solomon. 1709. *An Appeal to the Learned. Being a Vindication of the Right of Visible Saints to the Lords Supper, Though They Be Destitute of a Saving Work of God's Spirit on Their Hearts: Against the Exceptions of Mr. Increase Mather. By Solomon Stoddard, Pastor of Northampton.* Boston, MA: B. Green for Samuel Phillips at the Brick Shop.

—. 1700. *The Doctrine of Instituted Churches Explained and Proved from the Word of God by Solomon Stoddard.* London: Ralph Smith.

Stoever, William K. B. 1996. “The Godly Will's Discerning: Shepard, Edwards and the Identification of True Godliness.” In *Jonathan Edwards's Writings*, edited by Stephen J. Stein, 85–99. Bloomington, IA: Indiana University Press.

Strange, Alan D. 2003. "Jonathan Edwards on Visible Sainthood: The Communion Controversy in Northampton." *Mid-America Journal of Theology* 97–138.

Sweeney, Douglas A. 2015. *Edwards the Exegete: Biblical Interpretation and Anglo-Protestant Culture on the Edge of the Enlightenment.* New York: Oxford University Press.

Sweeney, Douglas A. 2005. "The Church." In *The Princeton Companion to Jonathan Edwards*, edited by Sang Hyun Lee, 167–189. Princeton, NJ: Princeton University Press.

Thompson, Nicholas. 2013. "Martin Bucer." In *A Companion to the Eucharist in the Reformation*, edited by Lee Palmer Wandel, 75–95. Leiden: Brill.

Todd, Margo. 2002. *The Culture of Protestantism in Early Modern Scotland.* New Haven, CT: Yale University Press.

Trueman, Carl R. 1994. *Luther's Legacy: Salvation and English Reformers, 1525–1556.* Oxford: Clarendon.

Turrell, James F. 2013. "Anglican Theologies of the Eucharist." In *A Companion to the Eucharist in the Reformation*, edited by Lee Palmer Wandel, 139–158. Leiden: Brill.

Turretin, Francis. 1997. *Institutes of Elenctic Theology.* Edited by James T. Dennison jr. Translated by George Musgrave Giger. Vol. 3. Phillipsburg, NJ: Presbyterian and Reformed Publishing Company.

Vines, Richard. 1677. *A Treatise of the Institution, Right Administration, and Receiving of the Sacrament of the Lords-Supper.* London: Printed by J.M. for William Miller and Robert Boulter.

Vliet, Jan van. 2103. *The Rise of Reformed System: The Intellectual Heritage of William Ames.* Milton Keynes: Paternoster.

Wandel, Lee Palmer. 2006. *The Eucharist in the Reformation: Incarnation and Liturgy.* Cambridge: Cambridge University Press.

Watson, Thomas. 1668. *The Holy Eucharist, or, The Mystery of the Lords Supper Briefly Explained by Thomas Watson.* London: A. Maxwell for Thomas Parkhurst.

—. 1965. *The Ten Commandments.* London: The Banner of Truth Trust.

Webster, Tom. 1997. *Godly Clergy in Early Stuart England: The Caroline Puritan Movement c.1620–1643.* Cambridge: Cambridge University Press.

Willison, John. 1756. *A Sacramental Catechism: Or, a Familiar Instructor for Young Communicants. Plainly Unfolding the Nature of the Covenant of Grace, With the Two Seals Thereof, Baptism and the Lord's Supper.* Edinburgh: Samuel Willison and Company.

—. 1761. *A Sacramental Directory, or, A Treatise Concerning the Sanctification of a Communion Sabbath.* Fifth. Edinburgh: Sam. Willison and Matt. Jarvie.

—. 1756. *Sacramental Meditations and Advices for the use of Communicants: in preparing their hearts, and exciting their affections, on Sacramental Occasions ; and a Christian Directory, consisting of Forty Scripture Directions, proper for all those intending heaven.* Edinburgh: Samuel Willison.

Wolterstorff, Nicholas. 2013. "John Calvin." In *A Companion to the Eucharist in the Reformation*, edited by Lee Palmer Wandel, 97–113. Leiden: Brill.

Ziff, Larzer. 2013. *John Cotton on the Churches of New England.* Cambridge, MA: Harvard University Press.

INDEX

Below is a brief index of significant names and topics.

www.ingramcontent.com/pod-product-compliance
Lightning Source LLC
LaVergne TN
LVHW020627100826
845148LV00012B/2084
9781737902669